THE DIVINE COMEDY

BY

PHILIP FIRSOV

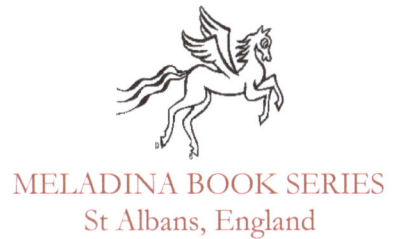

MELADINA BOOK SERIES
St Albans, England

Triptych

LA DIVINA COMMEDIA

After Dante Alighieri (c. 1265–1321)

Drawings: A1 (594 x 841 mm or 23.4 x 33.1 inch each)
2015, London
(in a Private Collection, London).

Engravings: A1 (594 x 841 mm or 23.4 x 33.1 inch each)
2016, London
(a few copies in some Private Collections)

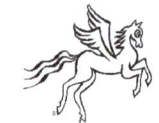

MELADINA BOOK SERIES
St Albans, England

Copyright © 2017 Philip Firsov, pictures and text

The book designed by © Dmitri N. Smirnov

ISBN-13: 978-1544276748
ISBN-10: 1544276745

Printed: CreateSpace
For Amazon
Charleston
USA

CONTENTS

Nel mezzo del cammin di nostra vita
mi ritrovai per una selva oscura,
ché la diritta via era smarrita.

Ahi quanto a dir qual era è cosa dura
esta selva selvaggia e aspra e forte
che nel pensier rinova la paura!

Tant'è amara che poco è più morte;
ma per trattar del ben ch'i' vi trovai,
dirò de l'altre cose ch'i' v' ho scorte.

* * *

Midway upon the journey of our life
I found myself within a forest dark,
For the straight-forward pathway had been lost.

Ah me! how hard a thing it is to say
What was this forest savage, rough, and stern,
Which in the very thought renews the fear.

So bitter is it, death is little more;
But of the good to treat, which there I found,
Speak will I of the other things I saw there.

Translated by Henry Wadsworth Longfellow, Inferno, Canto I

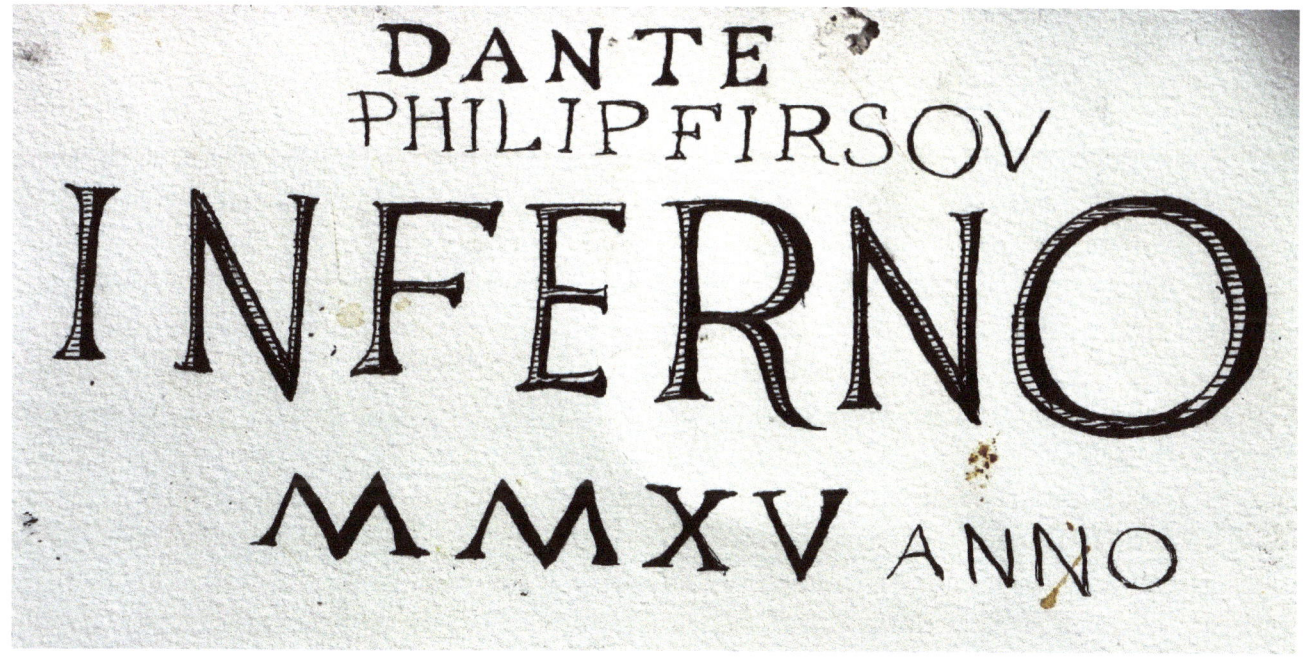

1. Inferno, title. Drawing.

LA DIVINA COMMEDIA

Philip Firsov: Illustration notes

INFERNO

In the middle of his life, Dante left the straightforward path and is lost in a dark wood. While he tries to climb a mountain he is chased by three beasts – a lion, a leopard and a she wolf. Virgil, the Roman Poet, appears as his guide and Beatrice, his platonic love, makes promise of reaching her in Paradise. Virgil takes Dante through the gates of hell where inscribed upon it are the words "abandon hope, all ye who enter here," to Charon's boat, where damned indecisive souls are beaten with an oar to board the boat to cross the river Acheron, beyond which are endless cliffs of descent into a crater formed by Lucifer's fall from the heavens. The conical structure of hell with its nine circles, some subdivided into nine Bolgias. Dante first encounters Limbo where pre-Christian figures lurk, unable to access the Christian Dominions of the underworld. These are Homer, Ovid, Horace and Lucan, followed by a castle of light containing Philosophers like Plato and Socrates and historic warriors. Minos stands at the entrance of the first circle. He then witnesses Harpies clawing suicides shoulders – these have deprived themselves of their human form and are engrained in trees with their skin turned into bark. Dante is then saddened by Paolo Malatesta and Francesca da Rimini's account of their tragic love and sees a whirlwind of swooping lovers in a state of perpetual lust. In the third circle there are gluttons sunk in mud and eternally pelted by hail. There are many such Contrapassi in the story whereby whatever one was guilty of in life, the opposite punishment is administered in Hell. Virgil placates the three-headed Cerberus and they pass the fourth and fifth circle of Hoarders and spendthrifts, the wrathful and the sluggish. They come to a high tower at the entrance to the underground city of Dis, where initially they are denied access by three Furies invoking Medusa. In the graveyard of this city, the Sarcophagi of groaning Heretics burn with protruding limbs. They speak to the Tuscan Farinata of the Florentine political tirade. In the sixth circle there is a stench around the tomb of Pope Anastasias, in the seventh circle a landslide. The Minotaur, guardian of the Violent, breaks into a fit of rage. Phlegeton, the river of blood is bubbling with souls shot by centaurs as they attempt to reach the surface. In the gloom of the wood of suicides they witness a hunt. Then, the Poets behold the realm of Usurers, Blasphemers and Sodomites under a rain of fire. They mount the beast Geryon – a personification of Fraud who has a man's head, snaky lions body and eagles wings like a Chimera who flies them over untrodden crags and glens into the eighth circle "Malebolge" full of naked Seducers, among whom are Hypocrites and Simonists forced to bear the weight of their crimes by being subjected to wearing Leaden cloaks. There are people with their heads turned backwards that cry a river of tears into their furrowed buttocks, and there are burning Soothsayers and Sorcerers and Thieves, forever struggling with snakes due to their occupied wrists in stealing during their lives. The Demon Malacoda forks Barraters in a lake of Pitch, and Dante meets Vanni Fucci – his contemporary who predicts Political strife in Florence. They then see Judas transfixed on the ground and crucified. Agnello, who bites Buoso, which causes them to metamorphose into snakes in a cycle of biting exchange. In the eighth Bolgia of the eighth circle they meet Ulysses to hear his story of the voyages and in the ninth circle Mohammad and his son Ali hacked by daemons with swords as they are guilty of being Inseminators of Discord, along with the French Troubadour Bertrand de Born who carries his own head. They talk to Gianni Schicchi of the Florentine family Cavalcante before being helped by giants to descend into the ice-lake Cocytus under the sound of Nimrod's horn. The logic is that it gets colder the further away from the sun and thus people's heads are frozen in the ice. Dante glimpses two heads – one feasting on the others' brain – Count Ugolino who was guilty of eating his own children. Across the Lake, Lucifer can be seen with his three heads chewing on Judas, and the two killers of Julius Caesar Brutus and Cassius. They climb down his back to the centre of the Earth and as gravity flips over the struggle up his legs into a cave where a path leads them on to the safety of the shores of Mount Purgatory.

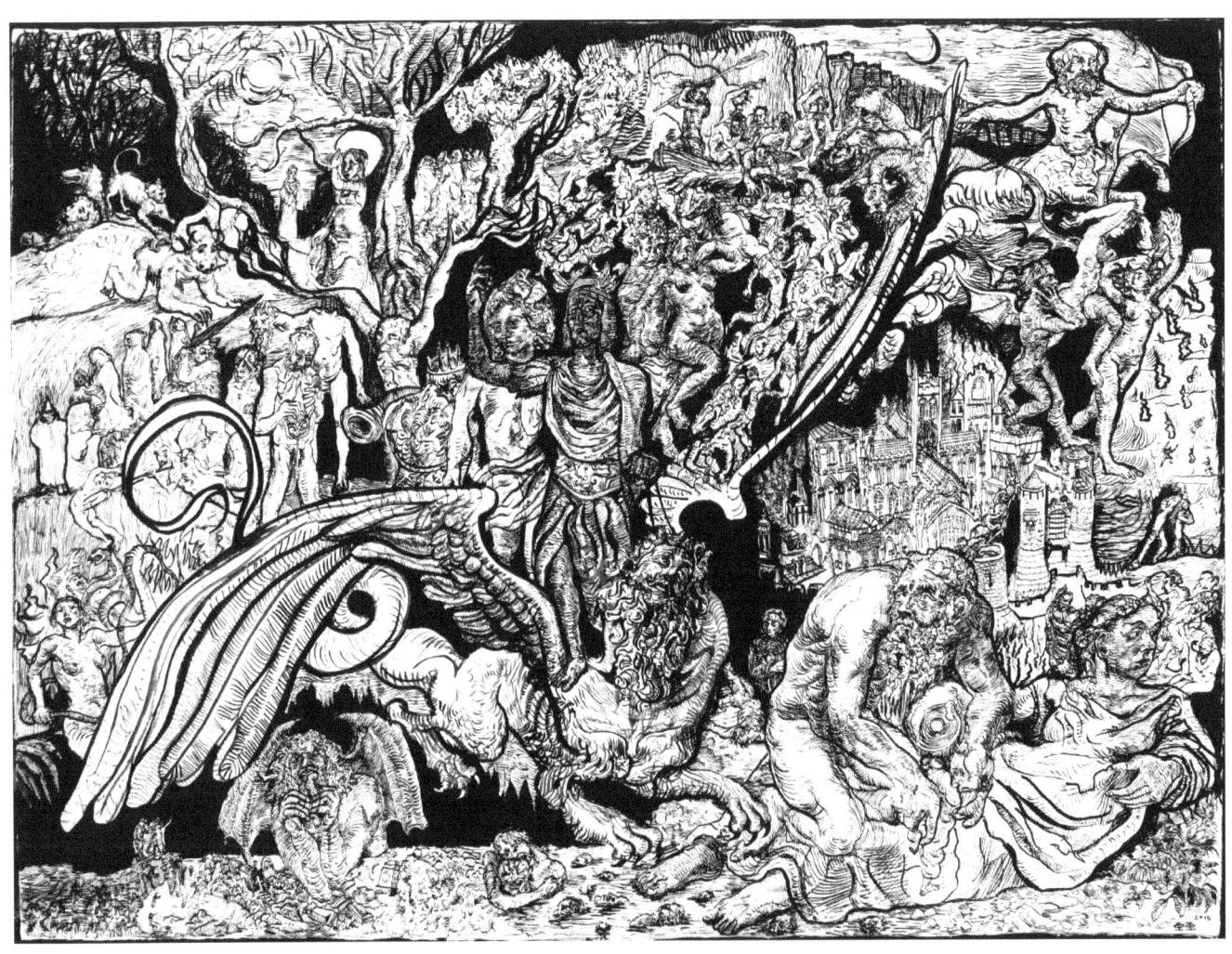

2. Inferno. Drawing.

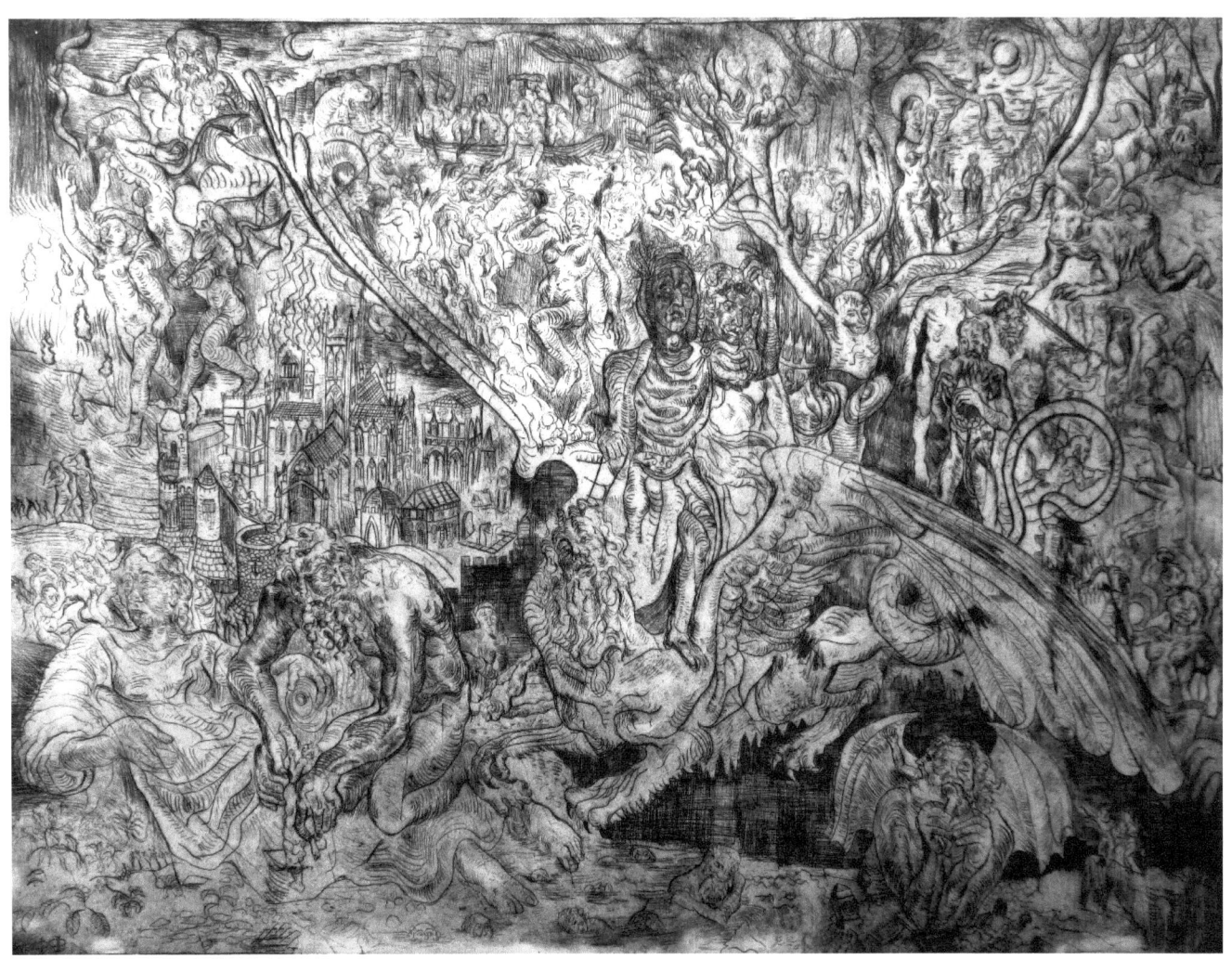

3. Inferno. Engraving.

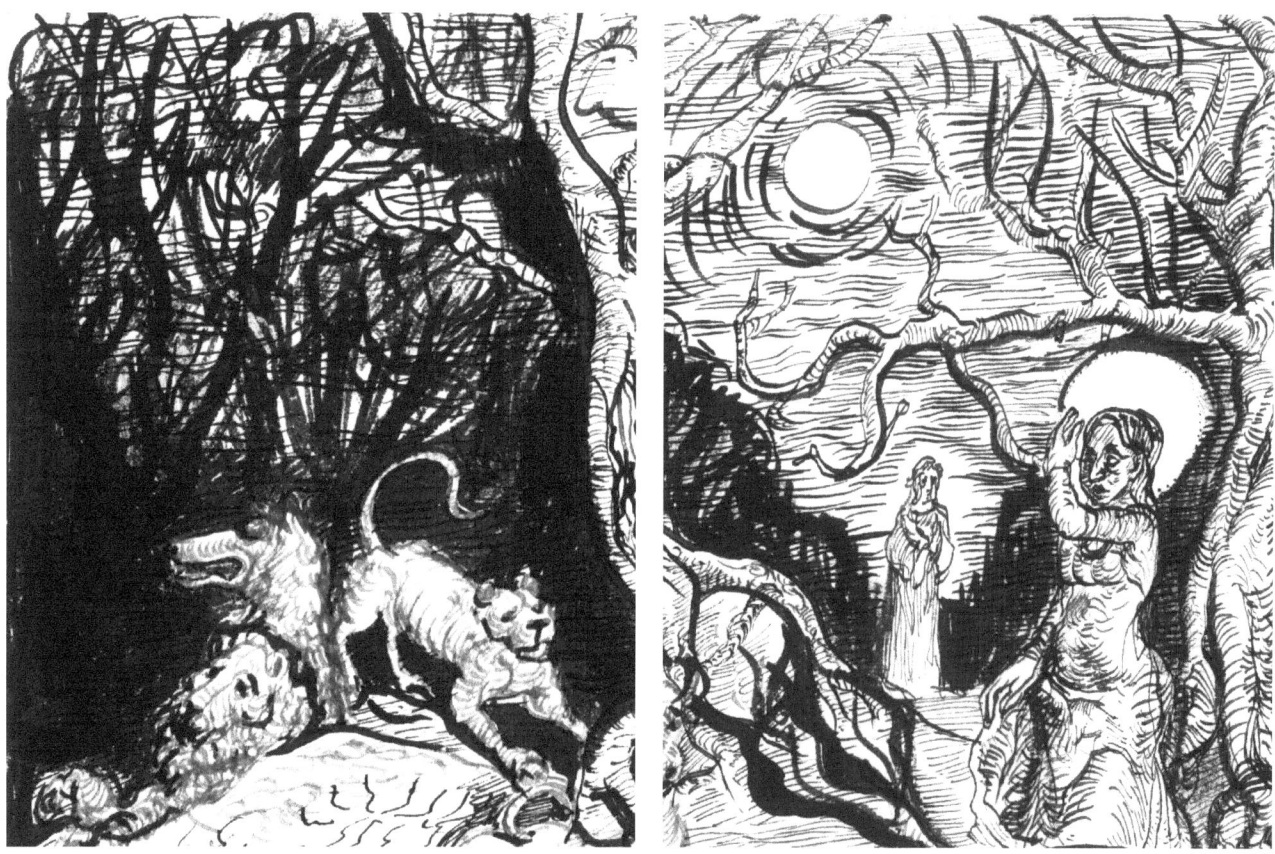

4-5. Canto I: a) Three Beasts: a leopard (pleasure), a lion (ambition or pride), a she-wolf (avarice); b) Virgil and Beatrice. Drawings.

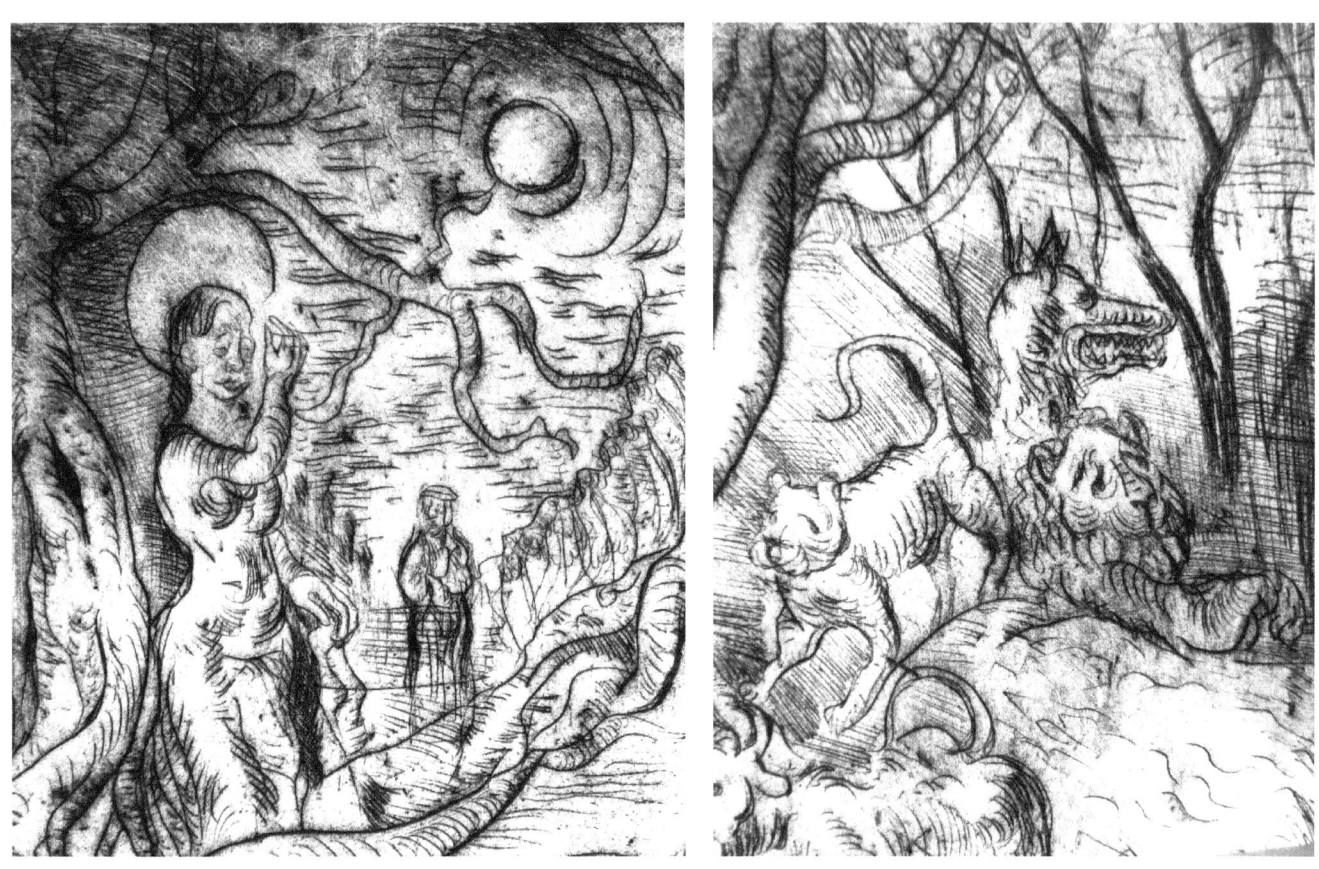

6-7. Canto I: a) Virgil and Beatrice and; b) Three Beasts: a leopard (pleasure), a lion (ambition or pride), a she-wolf (avarice). Engravings.

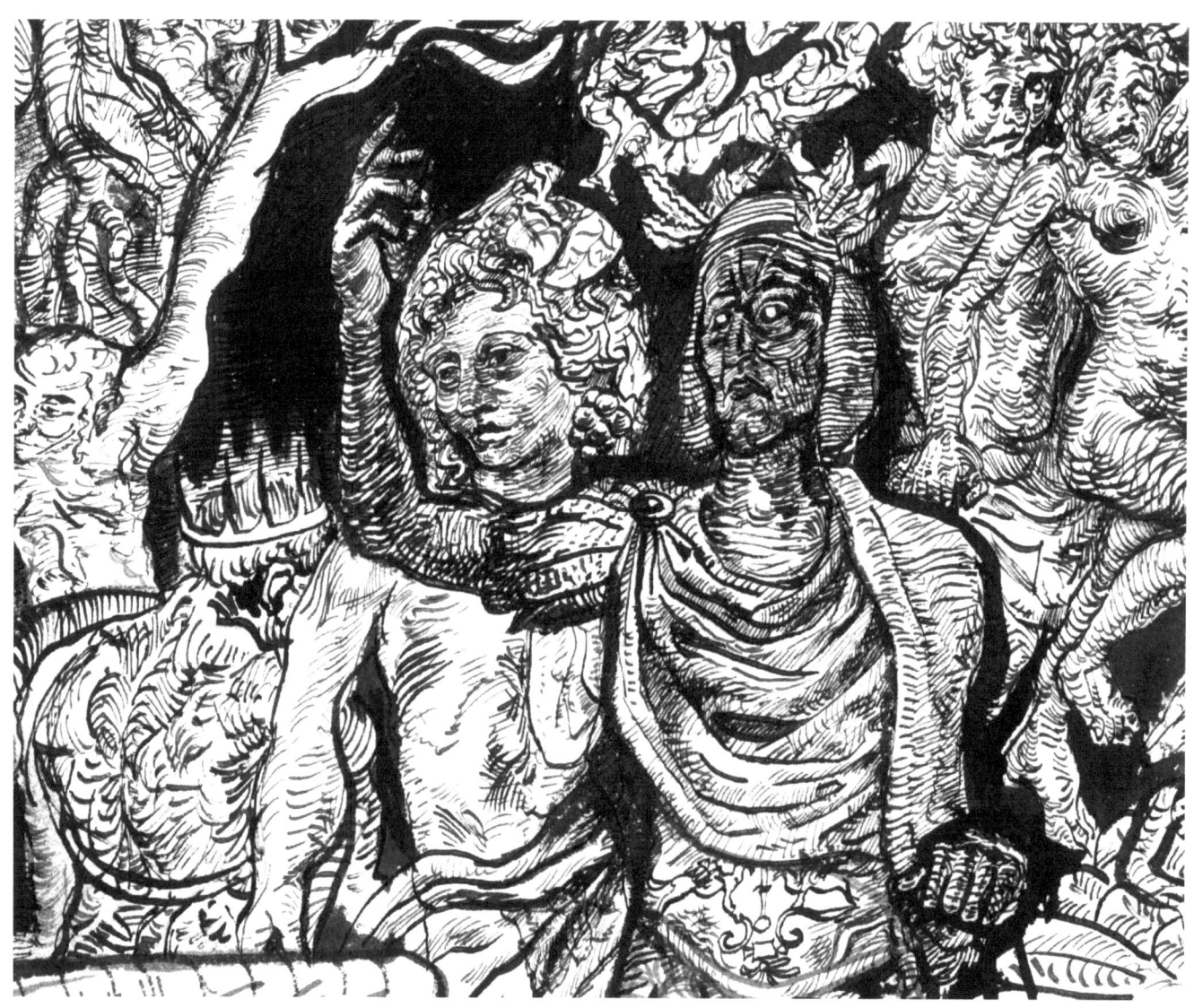

8. Dante and Virgil. Drawing.

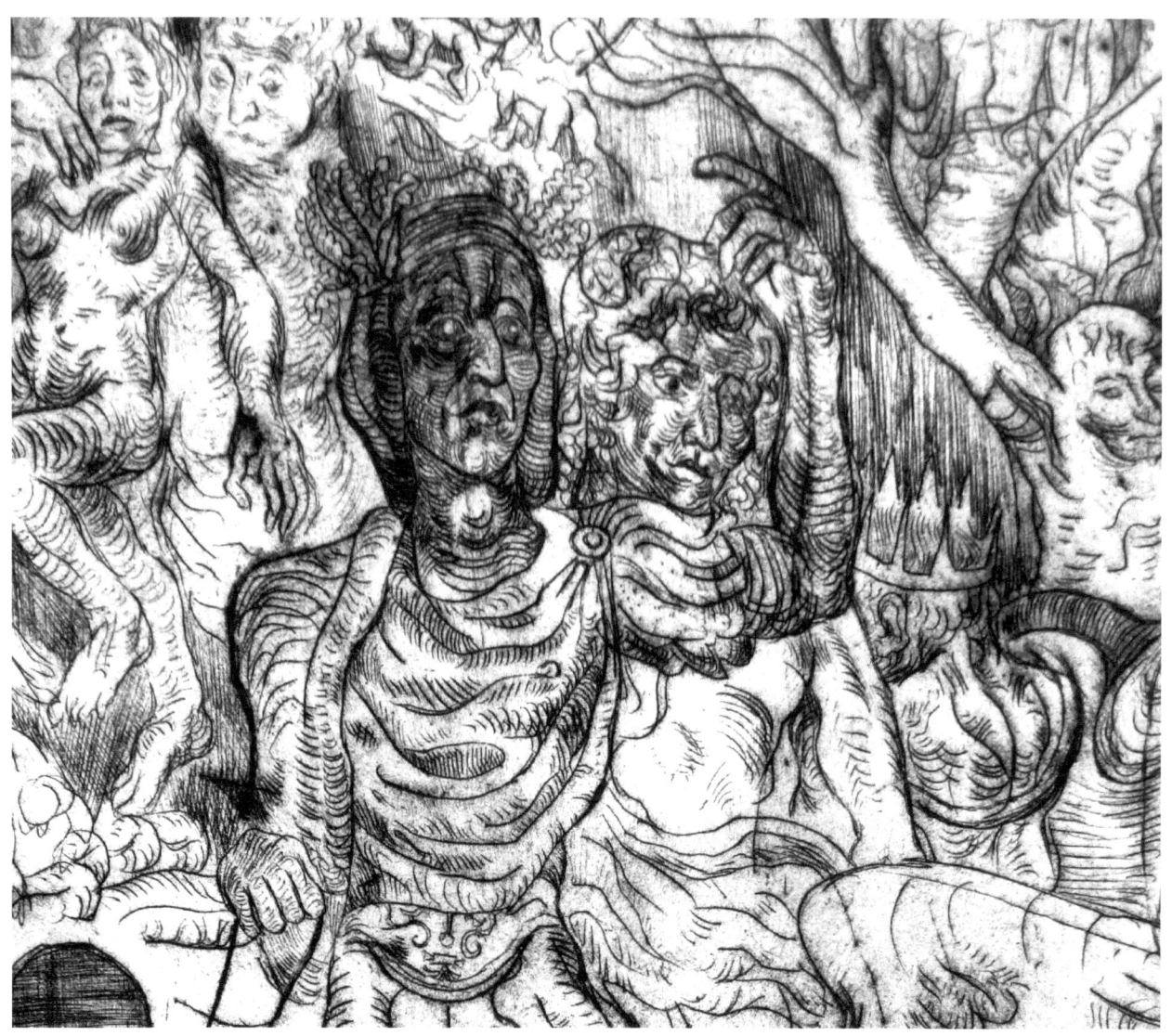

9. Dante and Virgil. Engraving.

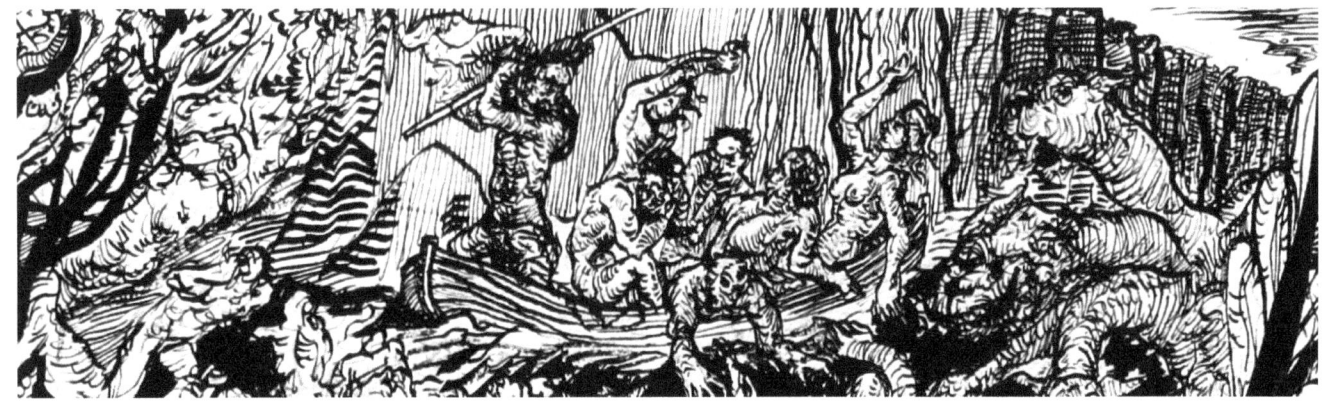

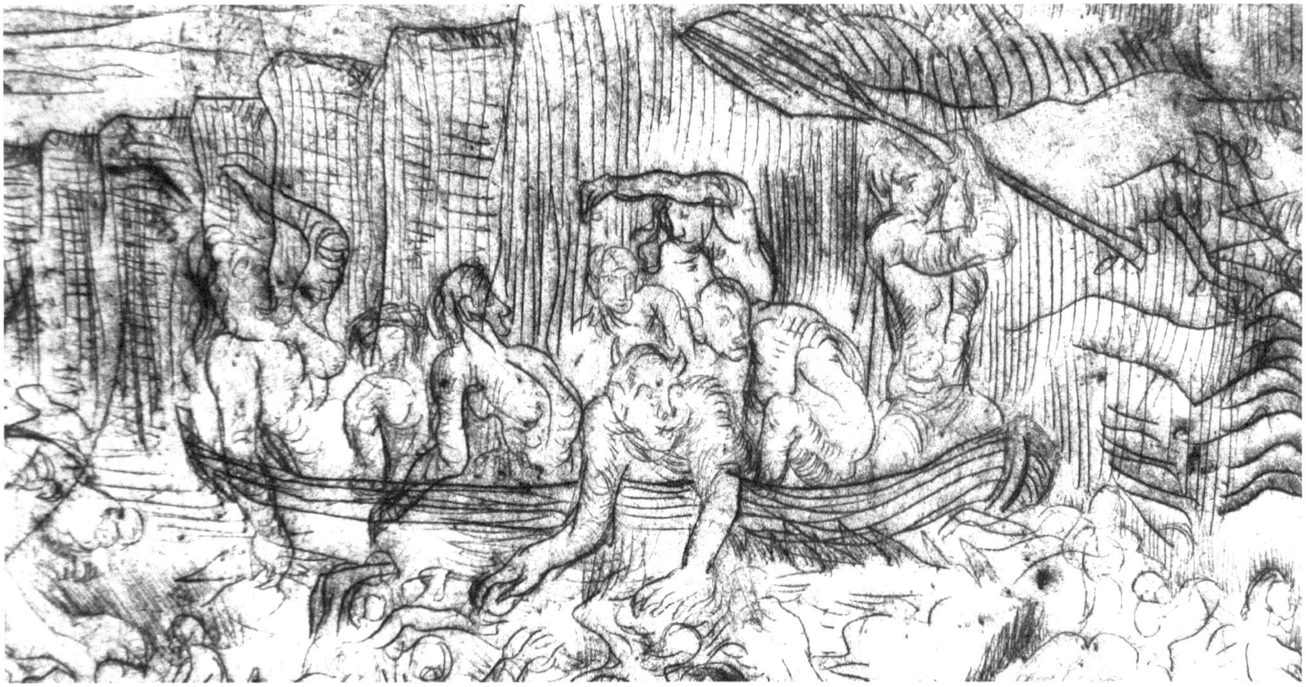

10-11. The boat of Charon. Drawing and engraving.

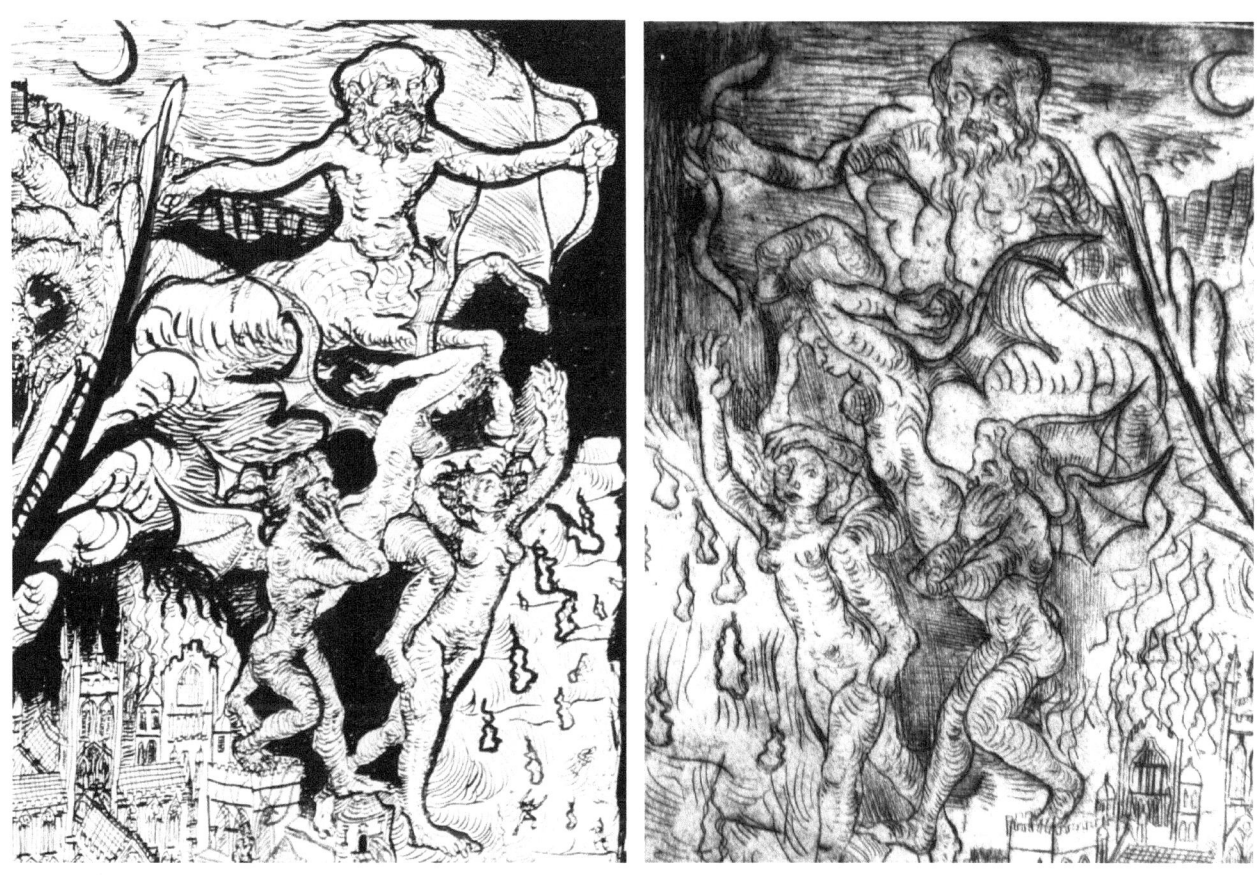

12.-13. Centaur and three Erinyes (or Furies): Alecto, Megaera, and Tisiphone.
Drawing and engraving.

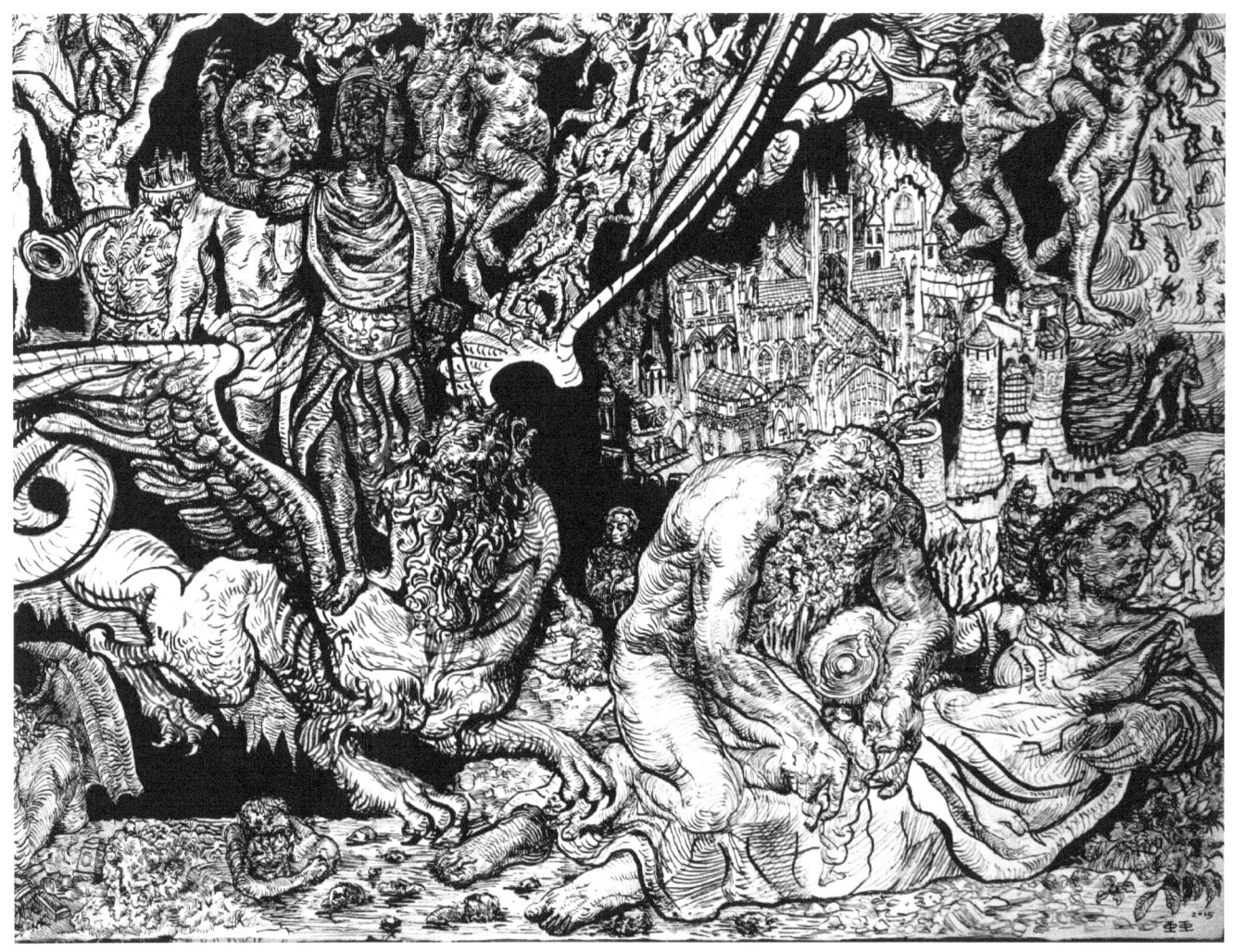

14. Nimrod with his horn, Virgil and Dante on Geryon's back, Paolo and Francesca among the whirlwind of the Lovers, the city of Dis, three Furies, the Giants, etc. Drawing.

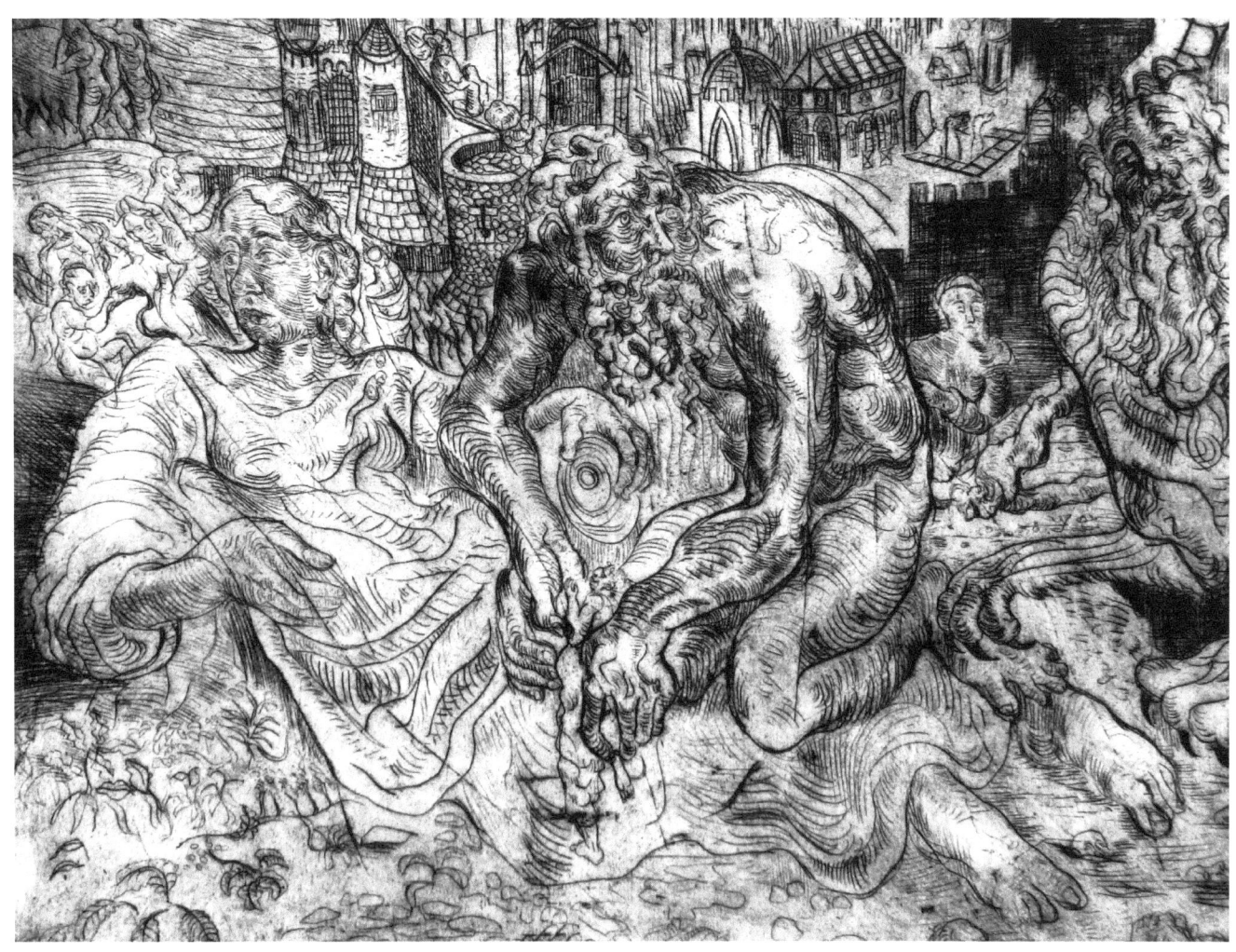

15. The city of Dis, the Giants. Engraving.

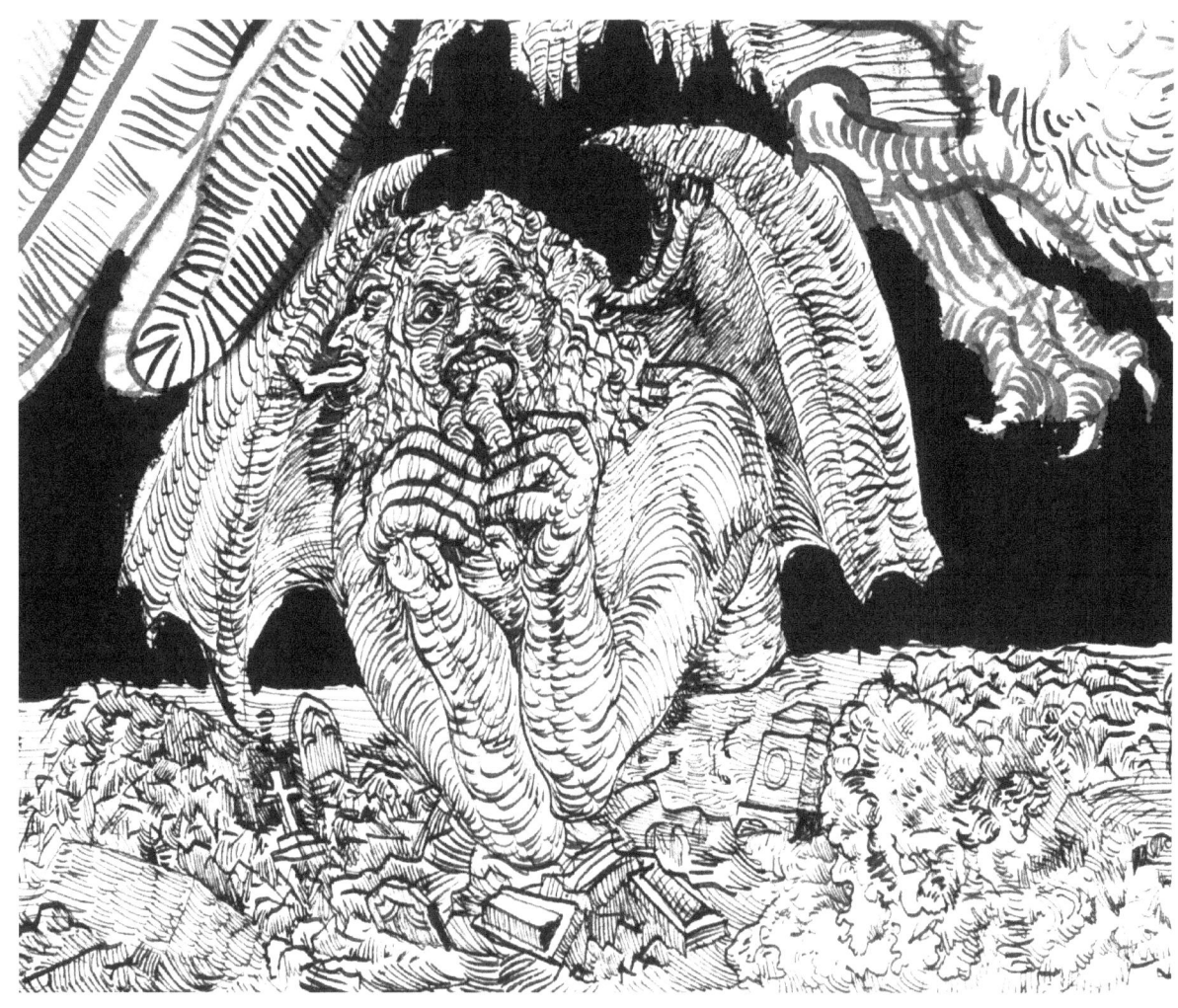

16. Lucifer. Drawing.

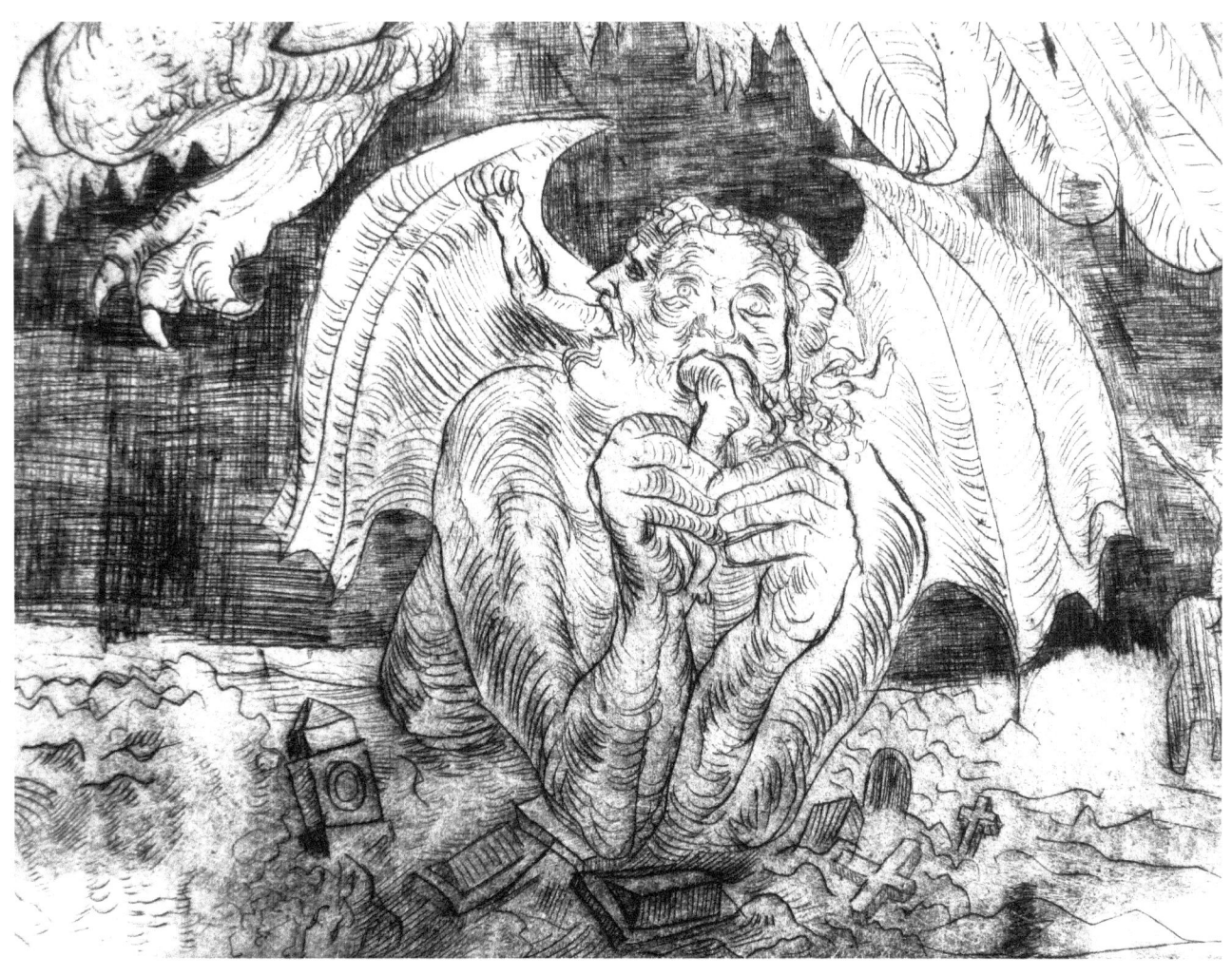

17. Lucifer. Engraving.

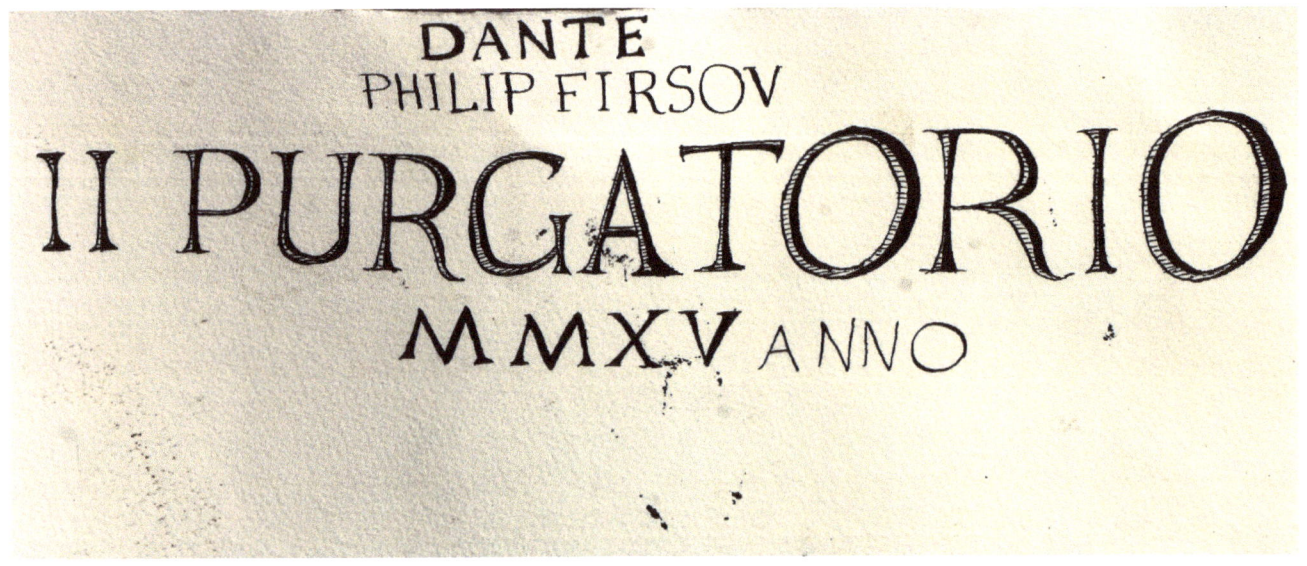

18.Purgatory, title. Drawing.

PURGATORIO

Having emerged from Hell Dante and Virgil find themselves on the Beaches of Mount Purgatory where they are met by Cato of Utica a Roman statesman and representative of stoicism, who is a political suicide and is in a different parallel type of ebbing Limbo. He directs them up towards the mountain and behind him they see a ship of souls piloted by a winged Angel under four stars. They sing the song "In exitu Israel de Aegypto". As they climb the slopes they see the procrastinating souls of the Excommunicated on the surrounding beaches and in grottos, above which as they climb a steep slope they witness the souls of the Late Repentant sing Miserere on a cliff edge. Here, Sordello the Mantuan troubadour acquaints them with the unshriven souls of Ante-Purgatory. They meet many Kings, princesses and knights and see angels flying with fiery swords, chasing away the Serpent from Genesis. The Blessed Ladies bear them up to meet the Angel of Peter's gate. He knights Dante and inscribes three "P's" representing sin on his forehead with the tip of his sword, and they can see their reflection in the steps made of different elements. Much like the legend of Icarus and Ganymede, Dante is suddenly flown up to the sun by a swooping eagle until his clothes catch fire before being laid down again. Beatrice is above in the sky beckoning him on in his doubts. Back on the foot of the mountain they reach the cornice of Pride, where they meet the bewailing Virgin Mary and Julius Caesar being redeemed. Guilty souls bear boulders up the mountain while there are also the envious including Arachne and Nimrod. Then the Poets clamber into a shelf of thick suffocating smoke, above which hovers the Angel of Zeal uttering the words "blessed are those who mourn" while there are blinded souls who refused to see sense, accompanied by an artist and a knight. In the fifth cornice they meet Hugh Capet and walk past many apathetic souls lying prostrate for five hundred years. They see little hope here and the lapidating of a soul drives them onwards. In the sixth cornice Gluttony is purged, as they behold a fruit lades tree too tall to reach with the sound of a voice droningly forbidding the souls to eat. Above this they pass through an embankment of flaming souls. Dante is urged on by Virgil to climb further until he reaches a sacred wood, where he finds singing Matilda picking flowers. The River Lethe causes rain and he crosses Eunoe – these are the two rivers of Oblivion and Remembrance. Matilda dips Dante into the water causing him to forget everything he experienced and then he is lead to watch a procession of three Virtues and Elders followed by a chariot borne by a half eagle half lion and a griffin, carrying the Giant and the Prostitute and he is told by Beatrice that he is at the Pageant of the Sacrament. Beatrice appears carried by angels and he is relieved of all his troubles. However Beatrice scolds him for having strayed from the true path of righteousness and salvation. Matilda plunges him into the Lethe to forget his sins thereafter and so, invigorated, he feels ready to finally ascend into Paradise.

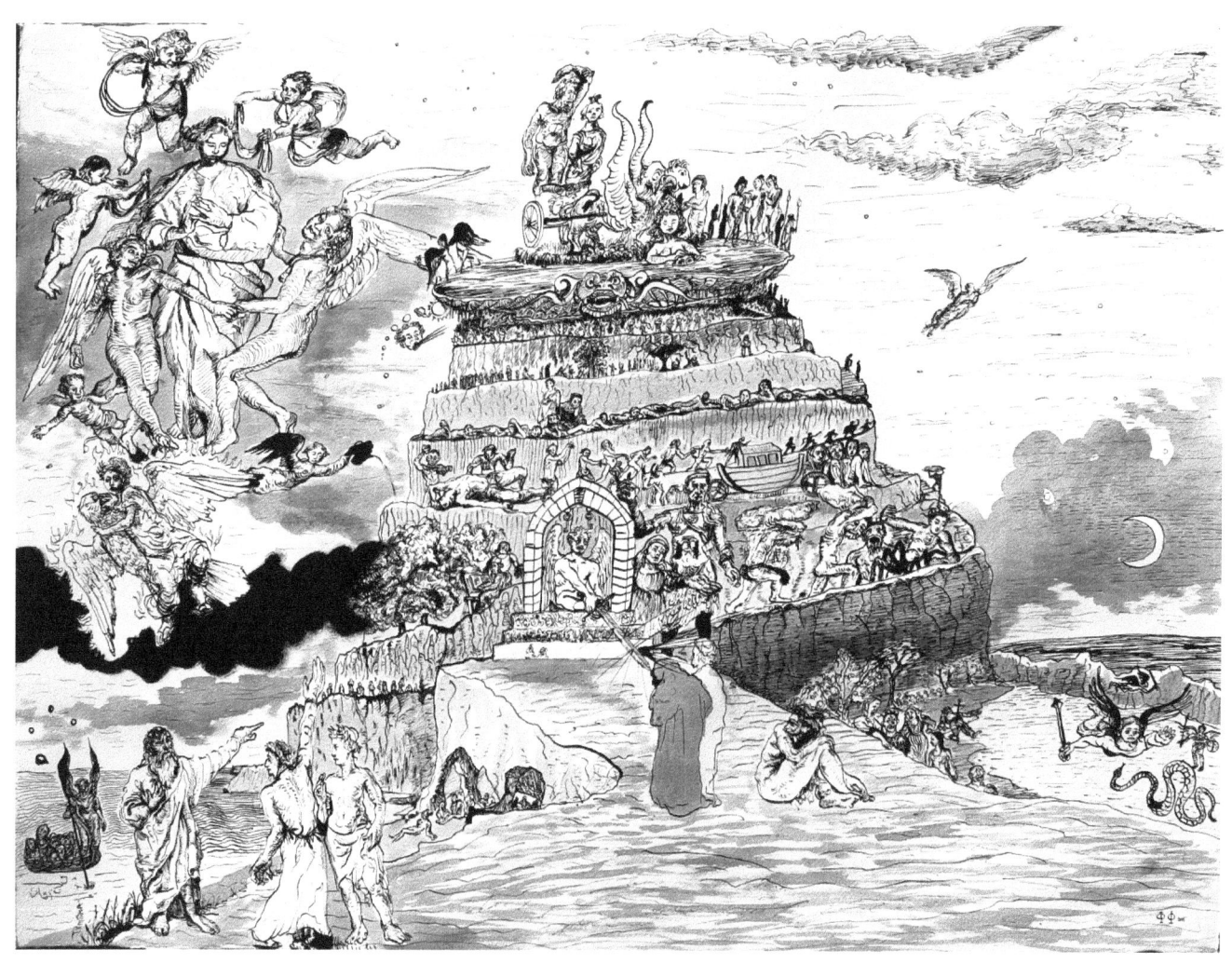

19. Purgatory. Drawing.

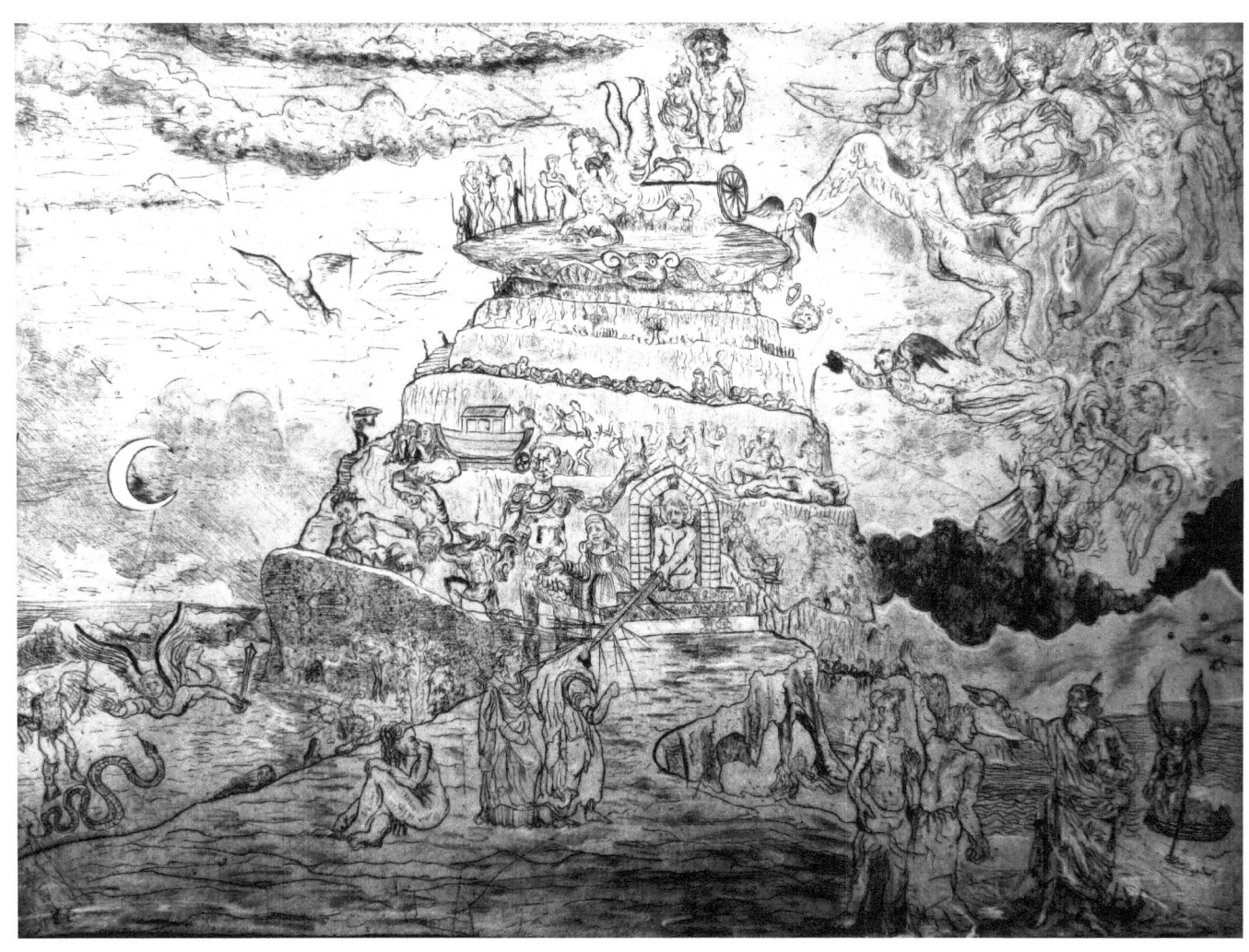

20.Purgatory. Engraving.

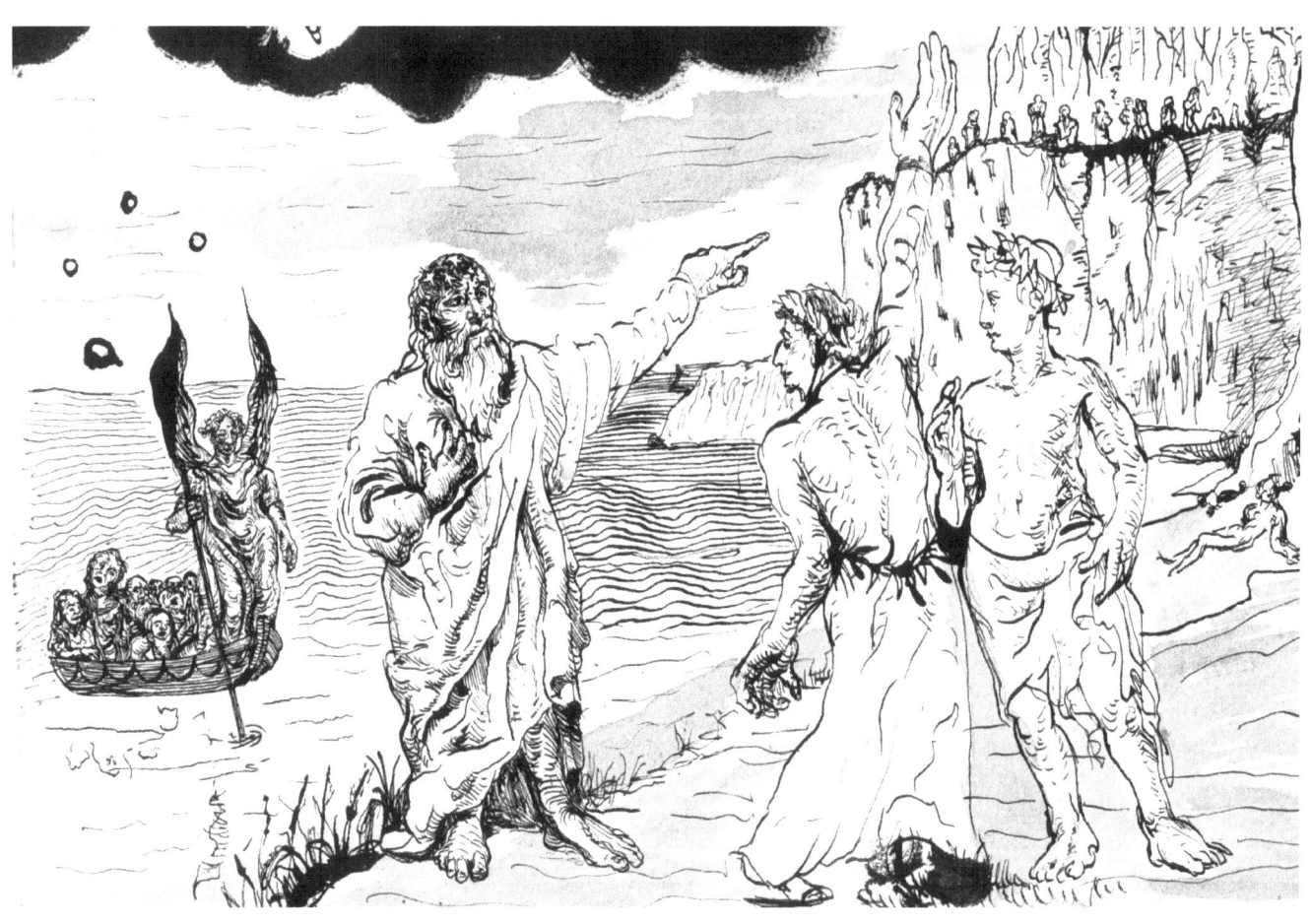

21. Cato of Utica with Dante and Virgil. Drawing.

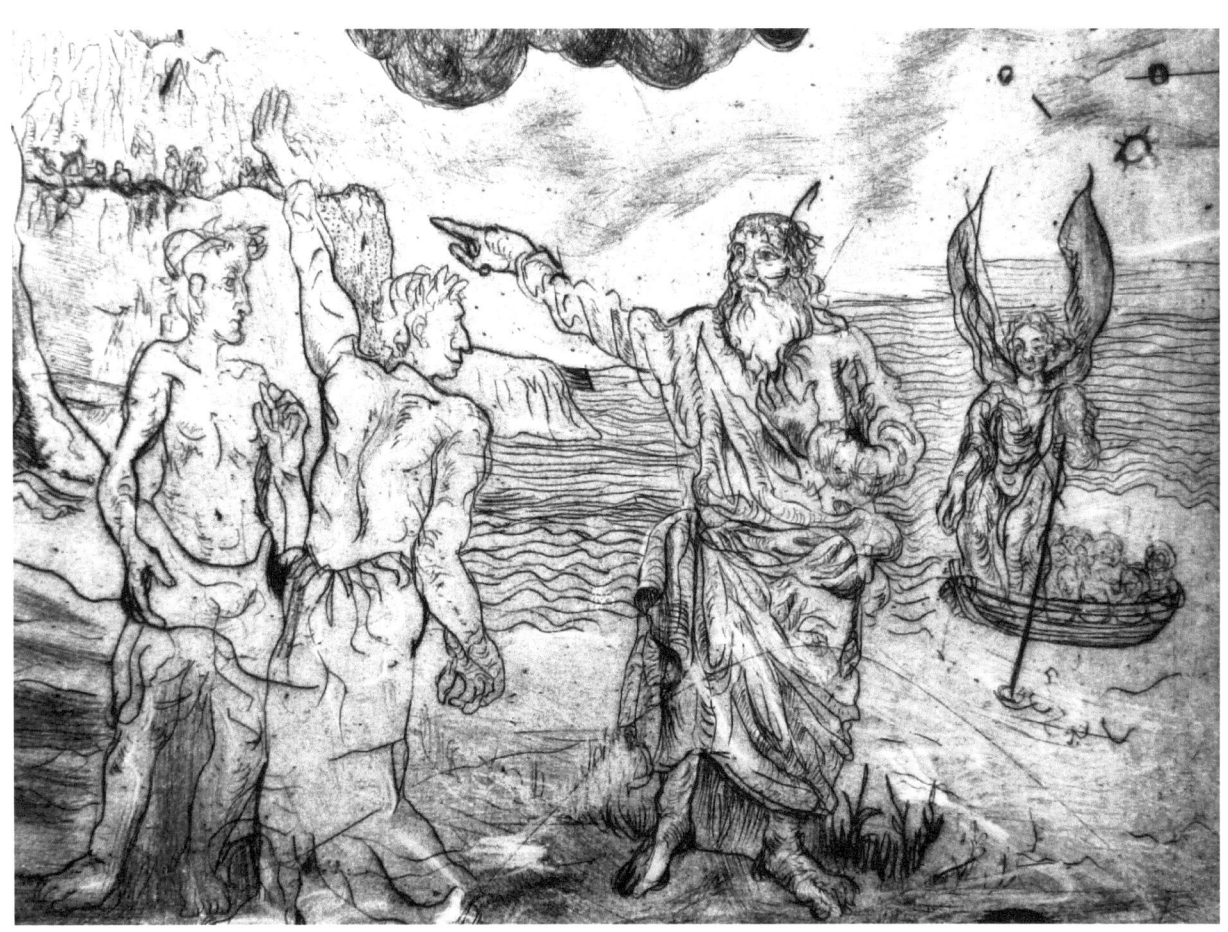

22. Cato of Utica with Dante and Virgil. Engraving.

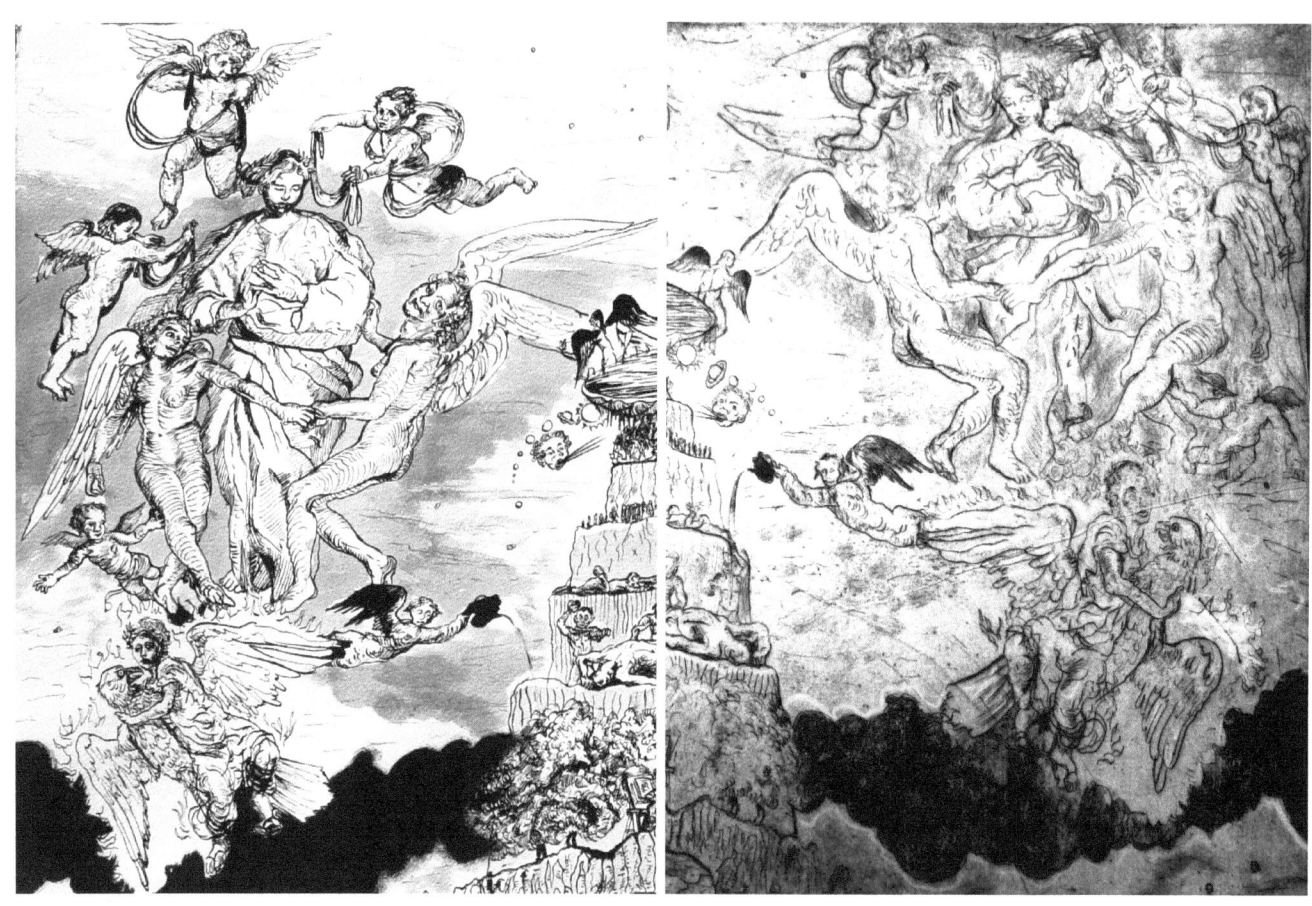

23-24. Beatrice. Drawing and engraving.

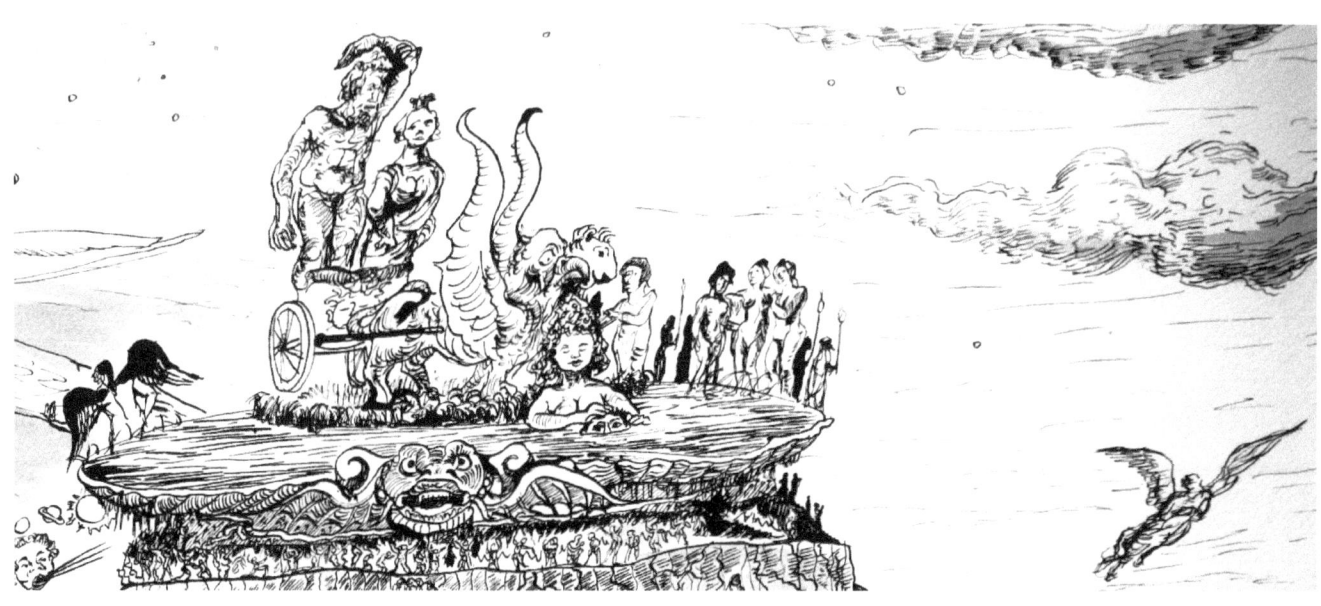

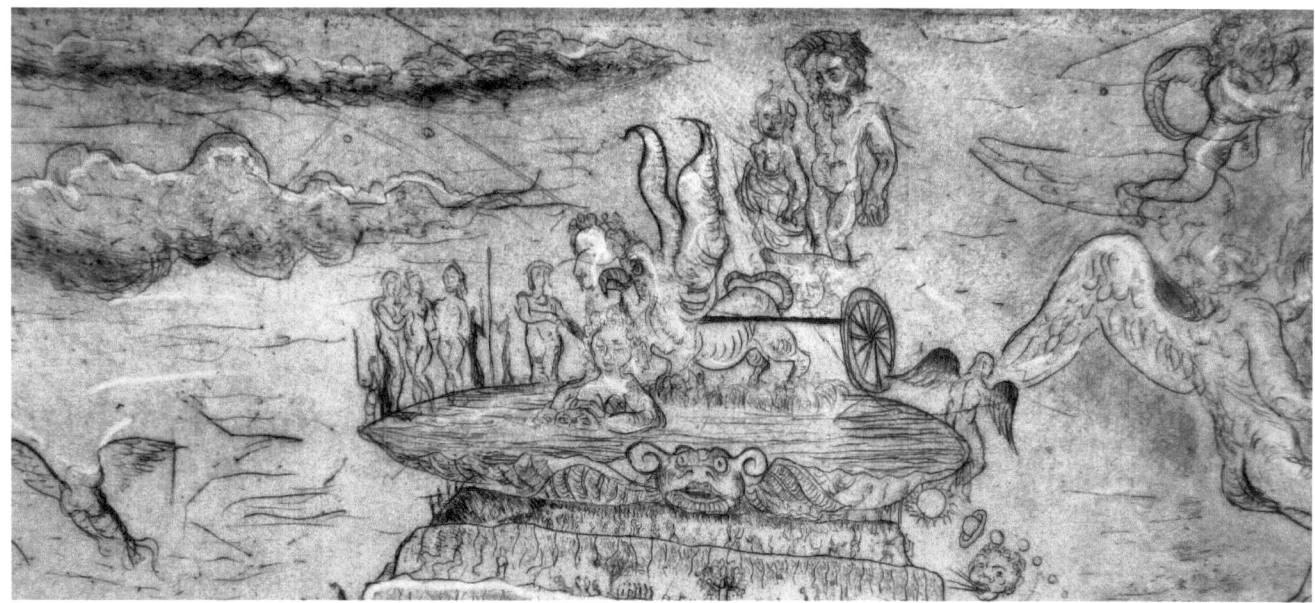

25-26. The Earthly Paradise At the summit of Mount Purgatory. Drawing and engraving.

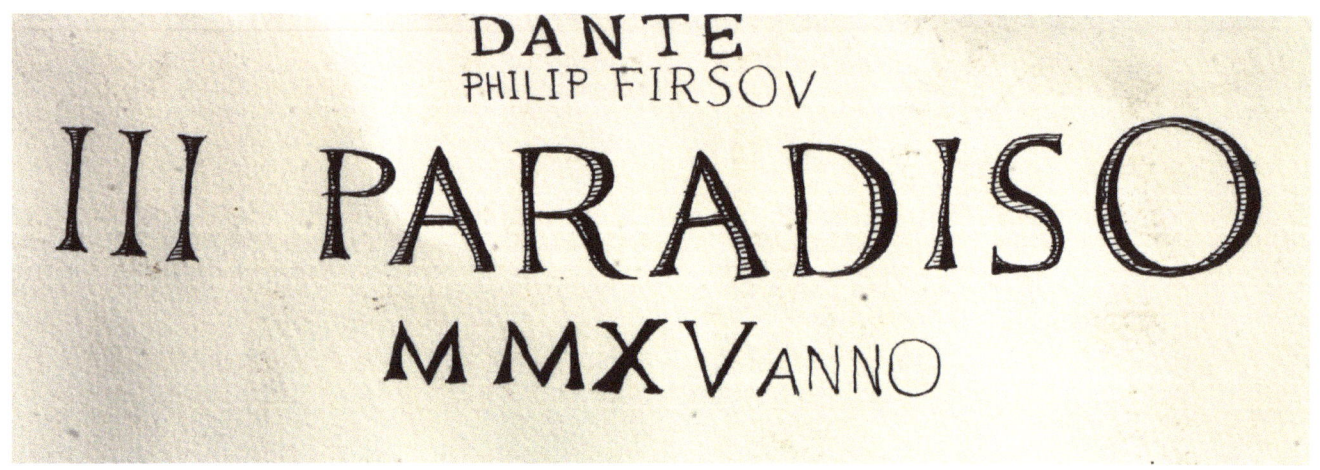

27. Paradise, title. Drawing

PARADISO

The final phase of the journey takes Dante through the ten Heavens. After drinking the water of Eunoe in the Garden of Eden with Beatrice by his side, he gazes into the midday Sun of the Equinox. He sees Apollo and hears the music of the Cosmos. They rise above the Earth like fish they float onto the Moon. Ghosts appear in pairs in a long queue among whom Dante talks to Piccardia dei Donati and the Empress Constance who both lead a life of celibacy but were removed from their nunneries by a contract of political marriage. Beatrice shines and answers his questions and eyes appear in space. Then they ascend to Mercury where crowds of luminous souls flock to them and Dante is able to question eminent Florentines and Byzantines. Then on Venus they see the city of Constantinople in its full glory. The fourth heaven is the Sun surrounded by clouds containing the souls of Saints and Leading Theologians and philosophers. Then they fly to Mars above which they behold a vision of the true cross carried by angels. On the red planet they meet Dante's ancestor emphasising the importance of Florence in the Heavens and discussing the lineage of the Alighieri family- he laments the lapsing of the glory days of the city state and its decline and Dante talks of the shock of exile. It is from him that Dante learns of his Banishment and how he will take refuge in the hospitality of Lord Can Grande in Verona. Then they witness tiers of angels circling Jupiter before an eagle formed of many angels' bodies materialises in front of them and their unanimous voices tell Dante of how complex the workings of the universe are and how a human mind is incapable of its comprehension. On Jupiter they meet the recording Scribe angel and tour the Holy land to see Solomon and King David. On entering Saturn they meet kings and saints around Catria – a mythological version of Tuscany and in particular an ascetic Saint Pietro Damiano who shows them Jacobs ladder where they see souls ascending to the Heavens. They meet Saint Benedict, the founder of Montecassino Monastery and then follow the ascending angels up the steps towards the realm of the fixed stars. Directly below, Dante can see the earth tilted to display in the same trajectory, the centre point of the Mediterranean Sea in line with Saturn. They look up at the sky's zenith in a vision of Christ triumphant, the mystic Rose of the Virgin Mary and the lilies of the Apostles. The angel Gabriel whisks her back to the Empyrean. St. Peter guides the souls of the Saints and Saint James arrives to talk of the meaning of Love. Also Saint James holds the holy city and staff and discusses Love and Adam reveals the nature of the fall and the date of Creation, as well as the language he spoke while on Earth and the length of his stay in Eden. Dante sees he is on a point above the Earth exactly between Jerusalem and Spain but Beatrice takes him up to the Primum Mobile – the crystalline ninth heaven. Here they discuss the origin of time and he sees God as a ball of light in the form of a Rose. This Rose is composed of many unfolding petals each containing a multitude of souls. God is surrounded by nine circles of concentric angels categorized into different named orders and Beatrice names the orders: Seraphim, Cherubim, Thrones, Dominions, Virtues, Powers, Principalities, Archangels and Angels. While gazing at the infinitesimal God, Dante questions Beatrice on the Creation and finds out that the Angels do not possess memory and see everything through God. The Angelic circles fade from sight and the White Rose of Paradise symbolizes divine Love. Dante bids Beatrice Farewell as she takes her place among the Angels redeemed. His new guides now are Saint Bertrand and the Virgin Mary, Queen of Heaven also borne on a cloud by angels and enthroned in the vault of the skies. He discovers the meaning of Love that "moves the Sun and other stars".

Philip Firsov, 2016, London

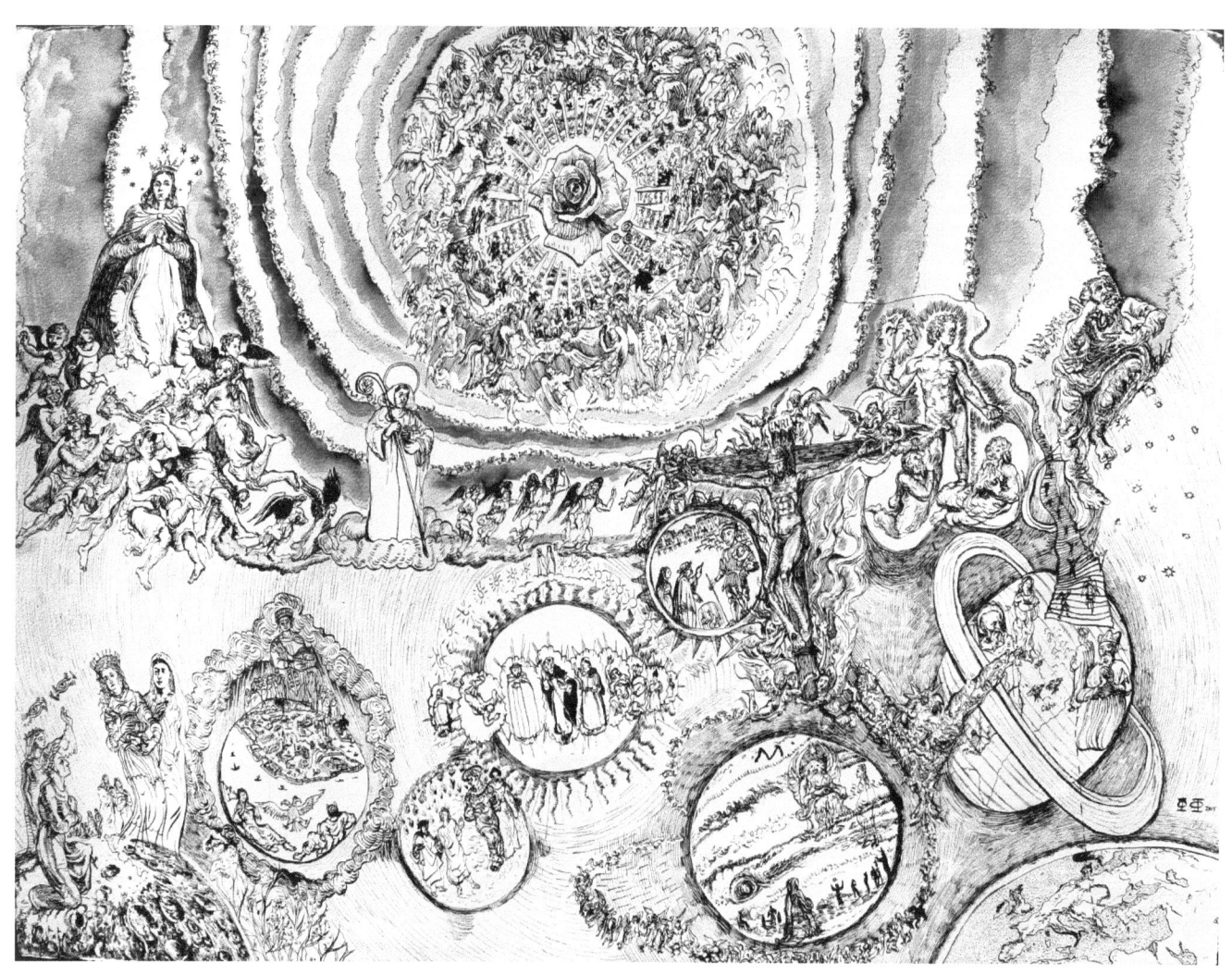

28. Paradise. Drawing.

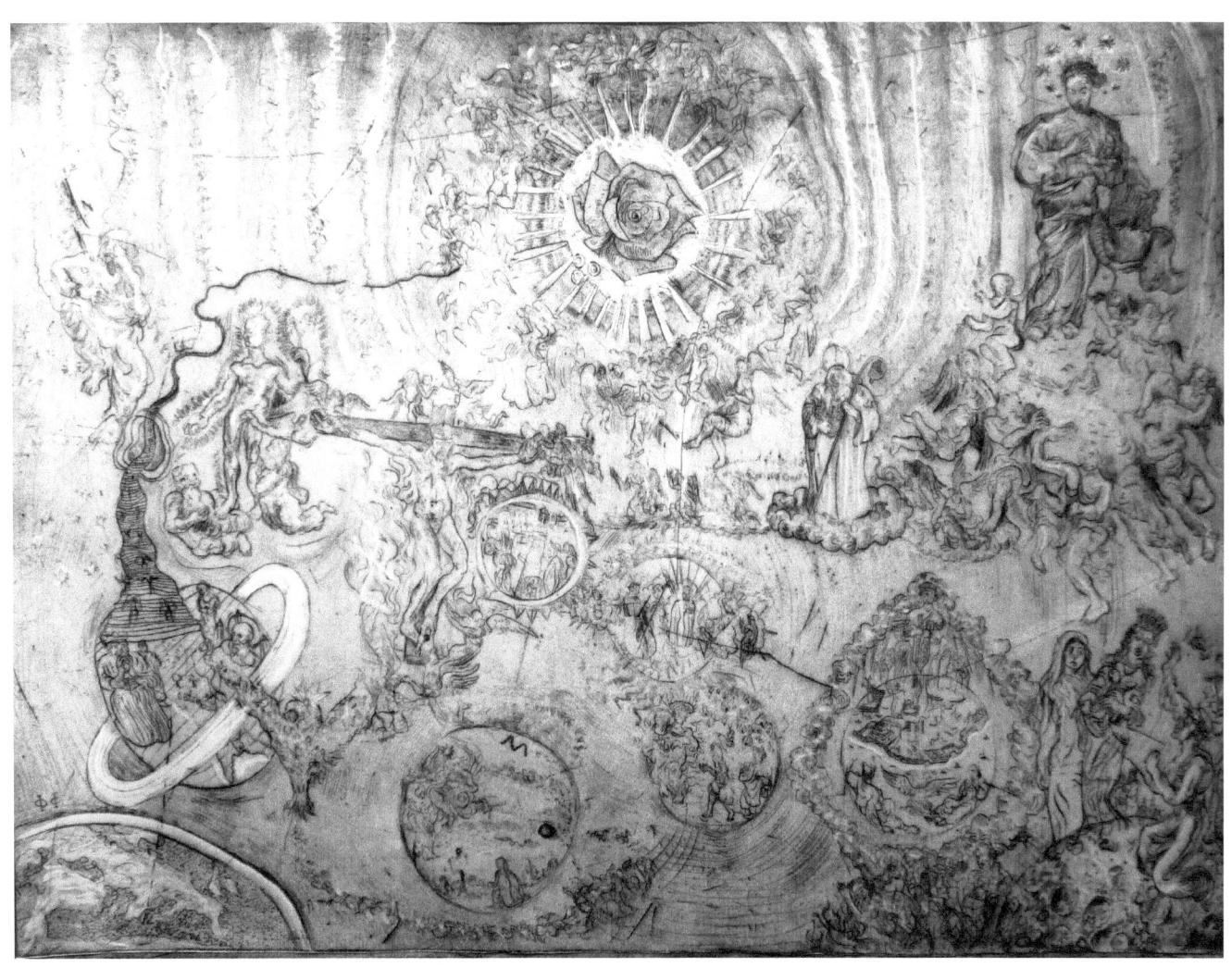

29. Paradise. Engraving.

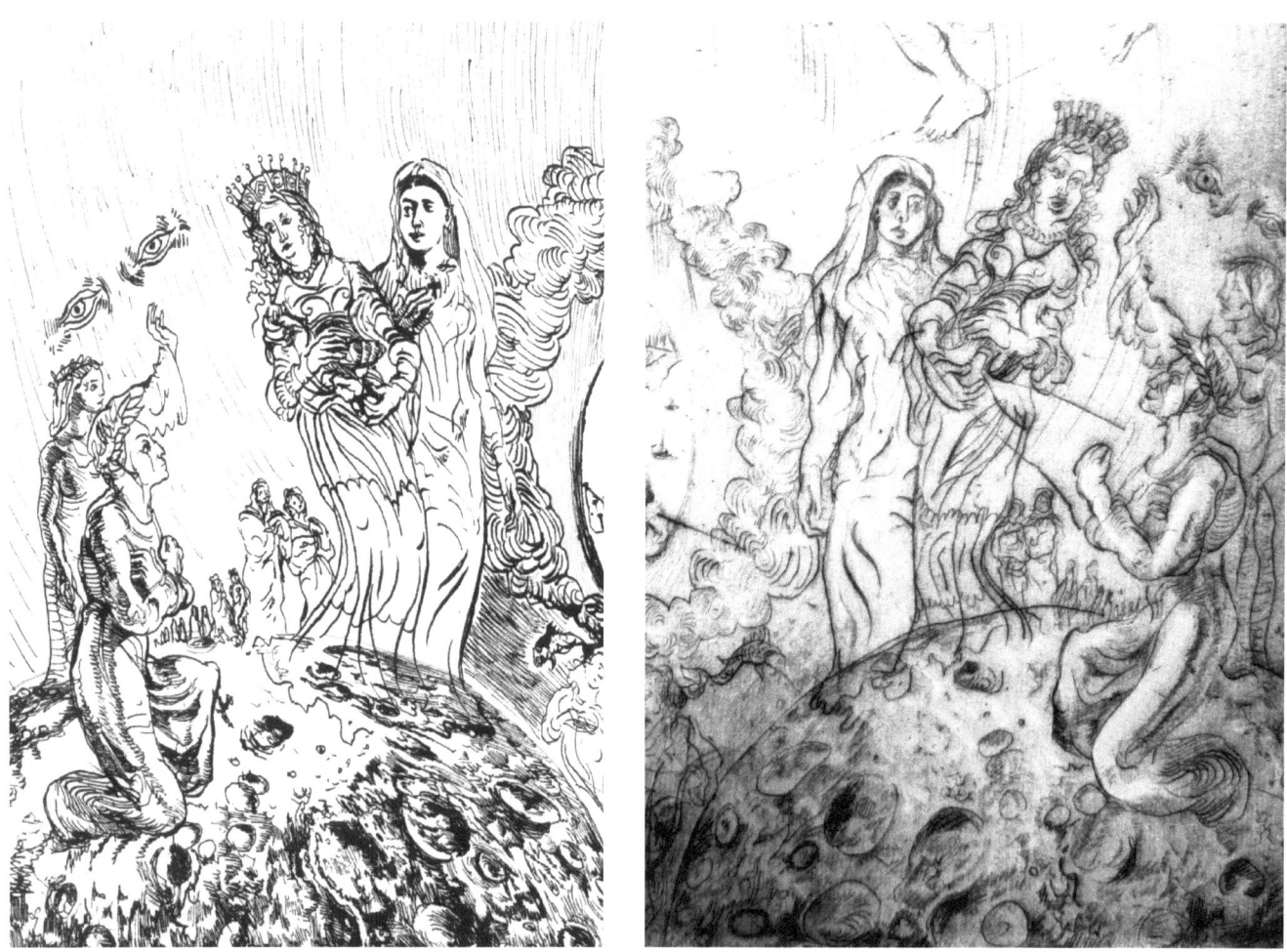

30-31. Dante and Beatrice arrive in the First Heaven, sphere of the Moon.
Drawing and engraving.

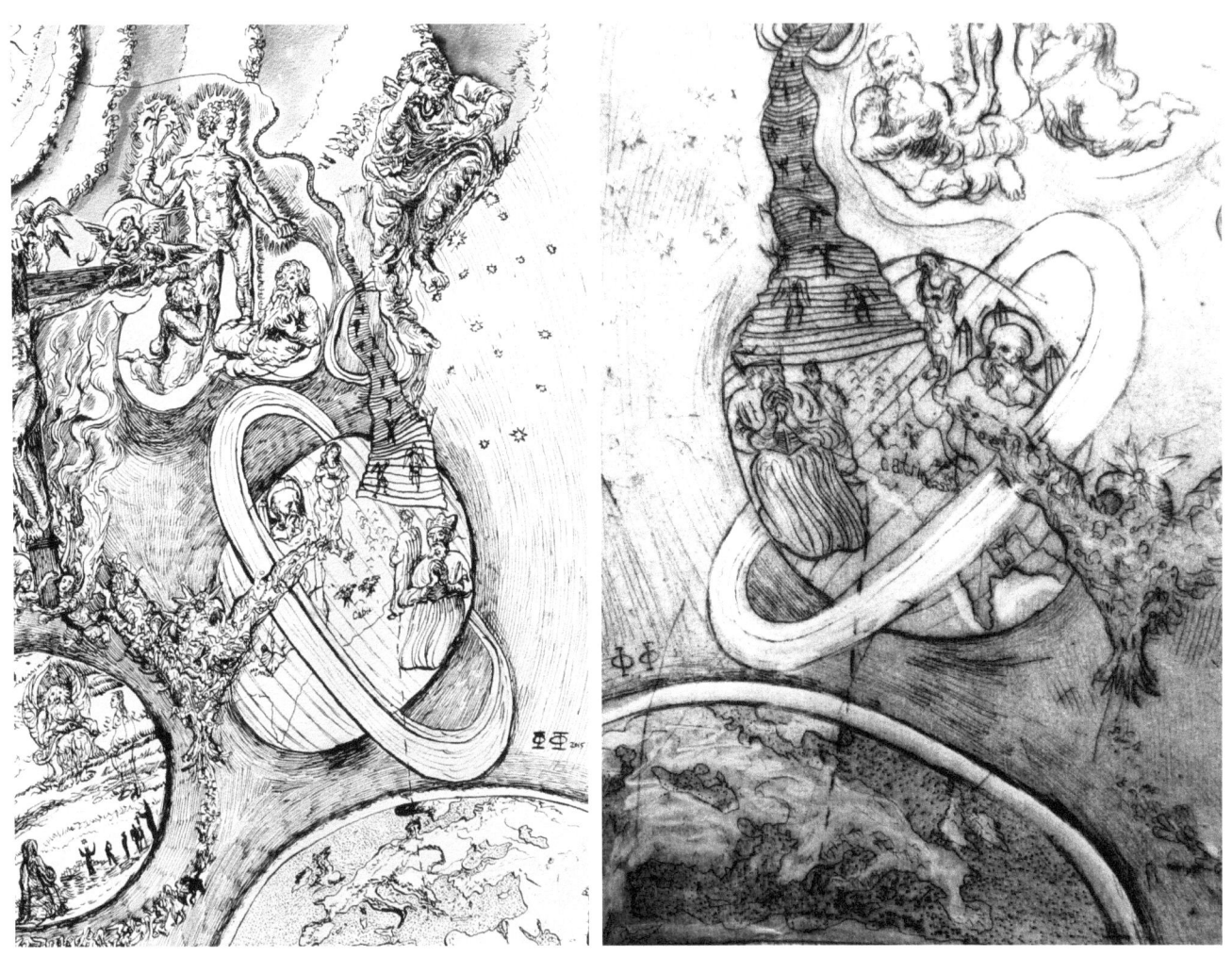

32-33. Saturn. Drawing and engraving.

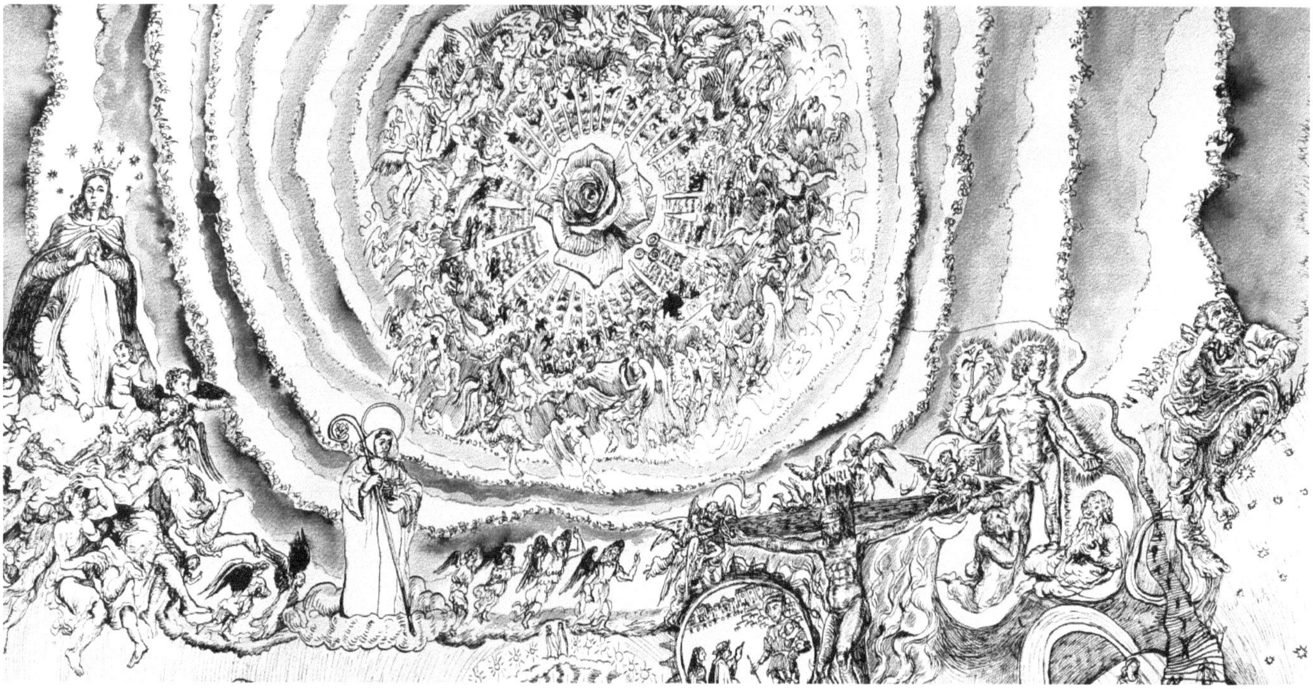

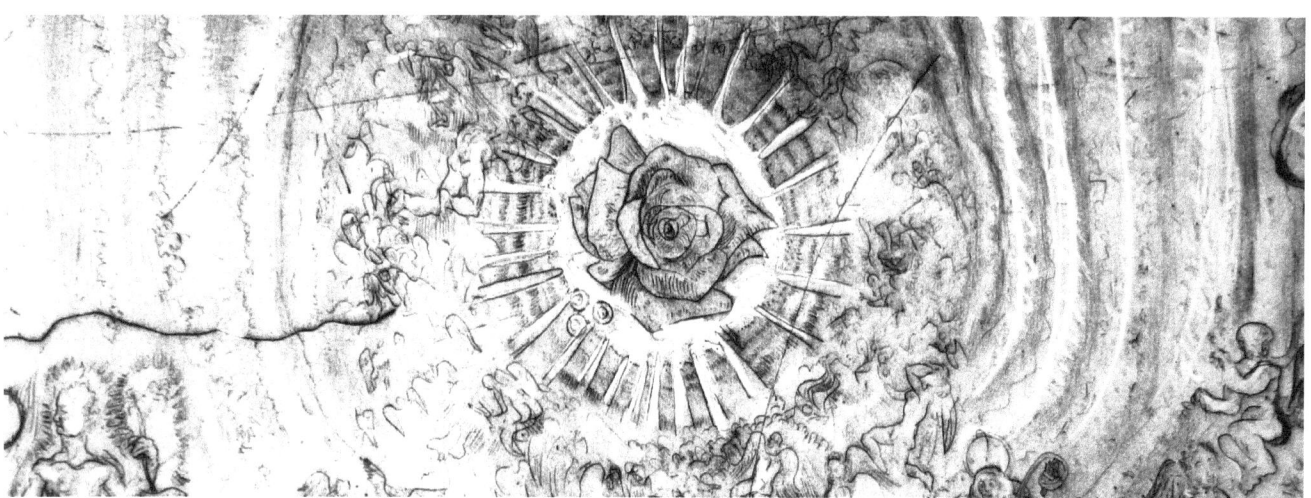

34-35. The Empyrean or the Heavenly Rose. Drawing and engraving.

tal era io a quella vista nova:
veder voleva come si convenne
l'imago al cerchio e come vi s'indova;

ma non eran da ciò le proprie penne:
se non che la mia mente fu percossa
da un fulgore in che sua voglia venne.

A l'alta fantasia qui mancò possa;
ma già volgeva il mio disio e 'l velle,
sì come rota ch'igualmente è mossa,

l'amor che move il sole e l'altre stelle.

* * *

…Even such was I at that new apparition;
I wished to see how the image to the circle
Conformed itself, and how it there finds place;

But my own wings were not enough for this,
Had it not been that then my mind there smote
A flash of lightning, wherein came its wish.

Here vigour failed the lofty fantasy:
But now was turning my desire and will,
Even as a wheel that equally is moved,

The Love which moves the sun and the other stars.

Translated by Henry Wadsworth Longfellow, Paradiso, Canto XXXIII

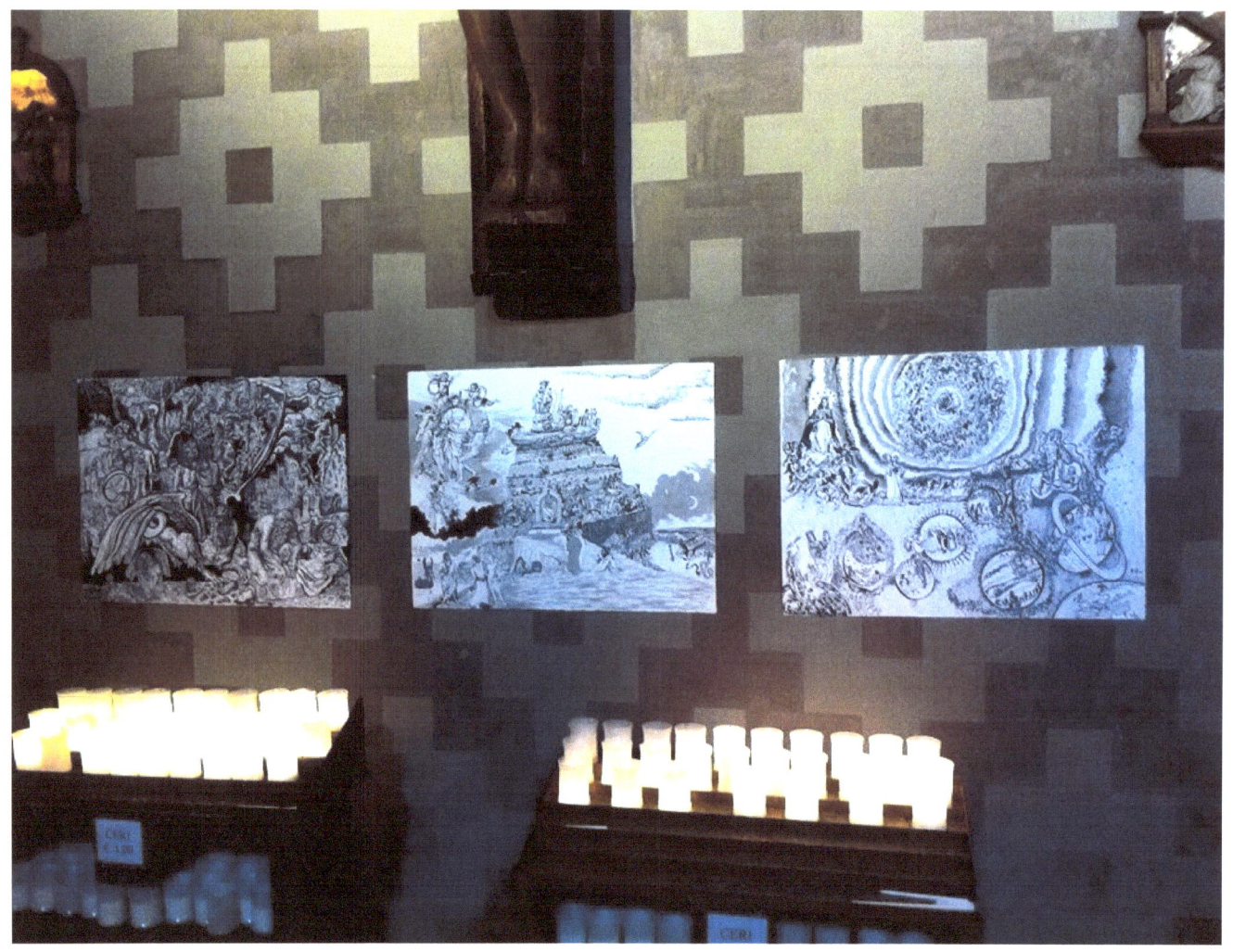

36. Exhibition of the Triptych in Asiago, Italy, 2015

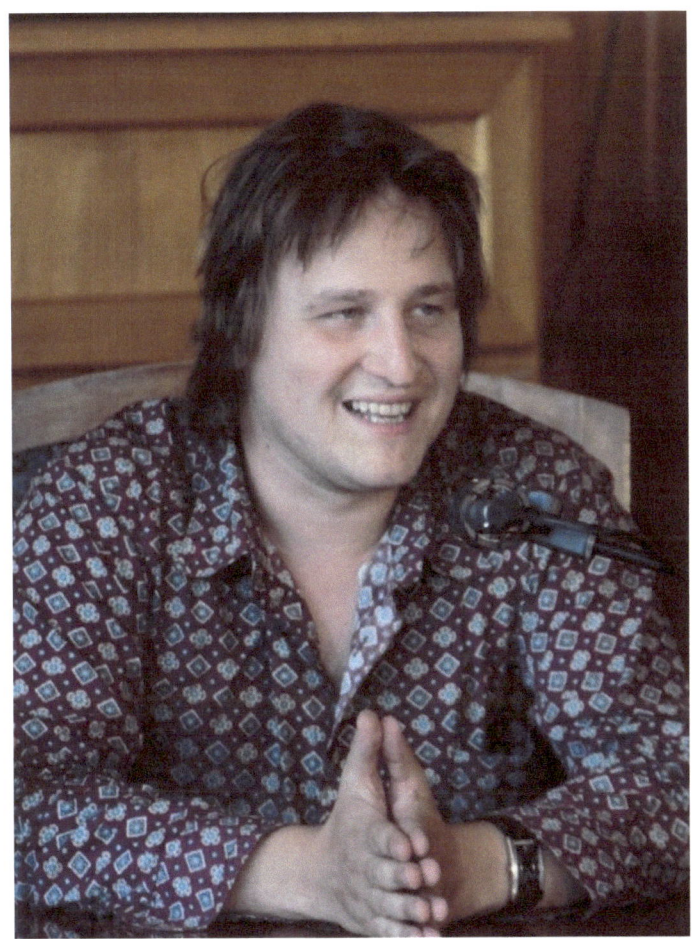 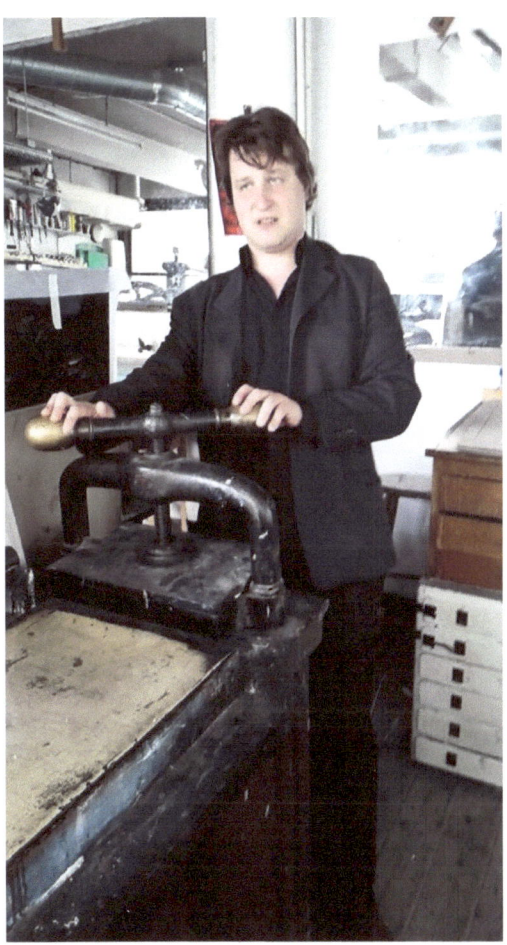

37. Presentation of the project, Asiago, 2015.   38. The process of printing, London, 2016.

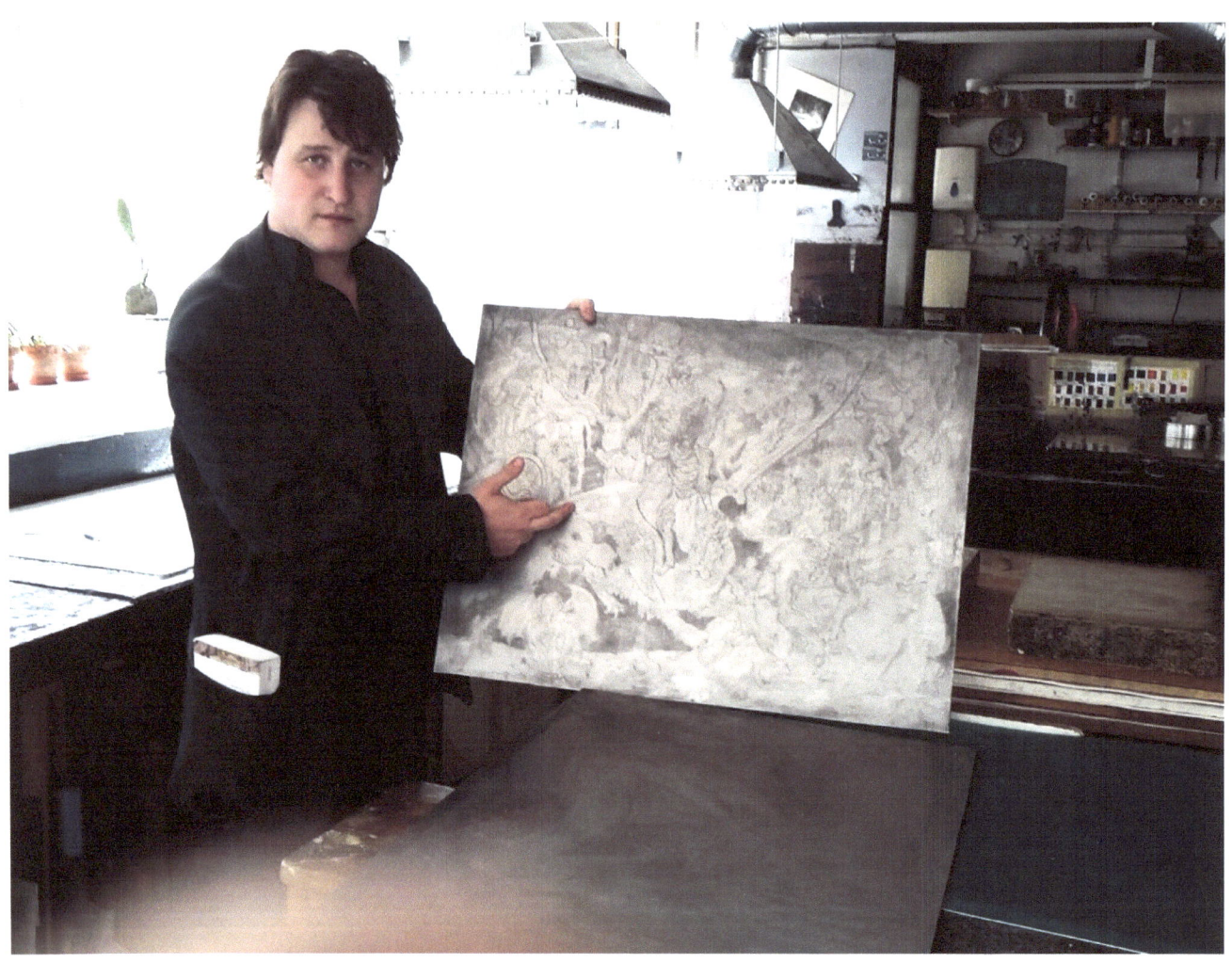

38. Philip Firsov with the aluminum printing plate of "Inferno", London, 2016.

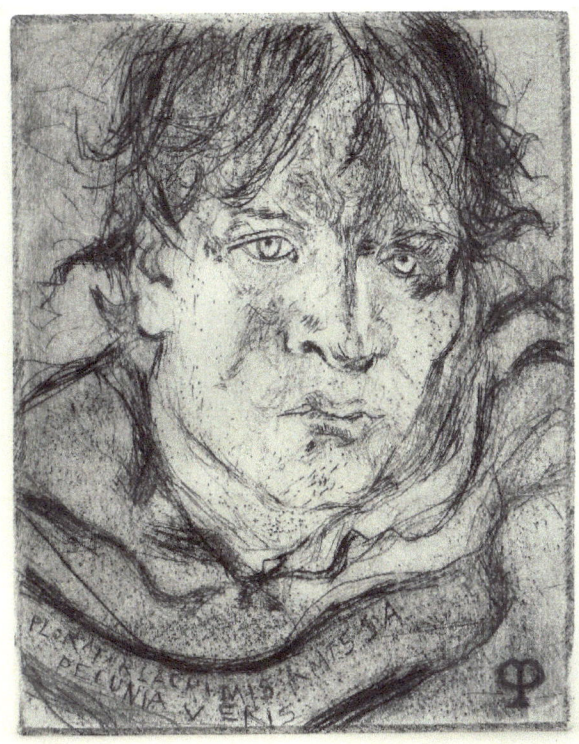

40. Self-portrait, 2009, engraving on a copper plate.

PHILIP FIRSOV

Philip Firsov is a British painter and sculptor of Russian origin. He was born on 8th of April 1985 in Moscow, into a family of two Russian composers, Elena Firsova and Dmitri N. Smirnov (pen name D. Smirnov-Sadovsky). Together with his family he left Russia at the age of six and settled in England (London). From the age of fifteen he studied art privately with Russian artist and restorer Alexander Kolesnik, and then continued his education at Central Saint Martins College of Art and Design (Foundation), Slade School of Fine Art (BA in Fine Art), and on The Drawing Year at The Prince's Drawing School (now the Royal Drawing School).